Wendy Taylor

Wendy Taylor

by Edward Lucie-Smith

Art Books International

First published in 1992 by

Art Books International
1 Stewart's Court
220 Stewart's Road
London SW8 4UD

© Art Books International Ltd

ISBN 1-874044-02-3

British Cataloguing-in-Publication Data.
Catalogue record for this book is available from
the British Library.

Design: Stewart Aplin
Editing: Judith Gray
Typesetting: Panic Graphics Ltd
Printing and binding: Toppan Printing, Singapore

Photograph credits
Bob Bell 81
Robin Campbell 129
Jan Chelbik 73, 74, 107, 122, 123
Roy Davis 117, 119
John Donat 1, 29, 33, 36, 38-41, 43, 44, 50, 55, 62-67,
69
Erroll Jackson 16
Mark Laidler 70
Nisbet & Wylie 137
Susan Ormerod 88, 131, 143
Andy Palmer 157
Positive Image 150, 153
Ray Tannen 3-6, 22, 25, 27
Charles Uht 13
David Williams 2, 11, 18-21, 31, 32, 34, 35, 37, 47, 49,
51, 52, 57-61, 76, 84, 85, 89, 94, 95, 97-106, 112, 128,
132, 133, 135, 138, 141, 144, 147-149, 155

All other photographs taken by Wendy Taylor.

Catalogue photographs by Roy Davis, John Donat,
Ray Tannen, David Williams and Wendy Taylor.

Sponsorship

Costain Building Products Limited of
Tallington, Stamford, Lincolnshire, a licensee
of Wendy Taylor's elliptical underpass
designs as produced for the Basildon
Development Corporation (see pages 79-82),
financially assisted Wendy Taylor in the
publication and promotion of this book.

*Additional sponsorship is gratefully
acknowledged from:*

Barclays Bank plc
L. T. Clark Limited
Milner Devaux Limited (Blanc De Bierges)
Redland plc
Rider Hunt & Partners
and a number of other generous sponsors

Wendy Taylor would like to express a sincere thank you
to all her family, Mick and Ted, Bruce and Matthew
Thomas, who have always been so supportive in so
many projects, and a particular thank you to studio
assistants, Terry, Andy, Mark and Olive, who suffered
many studio winters and fraught moments! She is
extremely grateful for the professional help and
expertise of the consulting engineers and teams who
helped make it possible to construct and site many of
the large-scale sculptures. While it is impossible to
mention the names of everyone who has been involved
over the years, their support will always be remembered
with gratitude.

PREFACE

Wendy Taylor is a phenomenon in the history of modern British sculpture. Not because she is a woman, however. Women artists in Britain, as elsewhere, have gained increased recognition in the years since 1945. She is unique because of the nature of her work – and also because of its wide dissemination and the frequency with which the public comes in contact with it. The probability is that she has more major sculptures on permanent public display in Britain than any other living artist. In the Britain of the 1970s she was one of the first artists to "take art out of the galleries and into the streets". Unlike other members of the same generation of sculptors, she did this without being interested in making ephemeral or impermanent work. The continuing theme in her career has been the making of large-scale, site-specific commissions, each piece meticulously engineered to withstand the conditions it was going to meet.

A number of her sculptures, among them her sundial by Tower Bridge, have acquired a powerful symbolic identity. **Timepiece** often appears prominently in the foreground of photographs which are meant to conjure up the image of modern London, a city rooted in tradition but looking hopefully towards the future. Significantly, however, the sculptor herself is seldom credited in the caption to the picture. Wendy Taylor's work is now so much part of the public consciousness that her own identity often seems to be concealed rather than revealed by the success of what she does.

One reason for this anonymity is that, at quite an early stage in her career, she made the decision to go directly to the public as far as possible. Her work is therefore seldom seen in commercial galleries, still less does it clutter up museum storerooms waiting to be rediscovered by some exhibition curator intent on illustrating a theme or a period of art. This fate – dignified semi-oblivion in the embrace of official institutions, but also a firm place in the reference books – is of course one which has befallen many of her contemporaries. By contrast, Wendy Taylor has remained highly visible as a creator of artworks, but much less so as a personality in the art world.

The purposes of this book are therefore very simple. Firstly, it chronicles a major sculptural career of the 1960s, 1970s, 1980s and 1990s. Secondly, it offers a link between a number of very familiar artworks and the person who created them. Thirdly, it attempts to explain the thinking behind these works which, though always logical, is often unorthodox. Looking through these pages, it will be seen that Wendy Taylor has never conformed to the stylistic norms of a given period. It is a minor subtext in her work that from time to time she seems to offer an ironic commentary on the artistic shibboleths of a particular moment, but it is perfectly possible to enjoy what she makes without being aware of this. Hers is a sceptical and individualistic art, but still more it is the work of someone who is passionately interested in art as a means of communication, and equally obsessed by the notion of appropriateness – to the site, the occasion, and the people responsible for the commission.

This book also demonstrates that Wendy Taylor's work is extremely various. For example, she is generally categorised as an abstract artist (though some of her apparently abstract pieces offer, on a second look, more than a hint of figuration). Yet she is at the same time an extremely gifted figurative draughtsman, whose drawings of animals form part of the great tradition founded by the eighteenth-century animal painter George Stubbs. Like Stubbs's work, these drawings are accurate, dispassionate, unsentimental, and also filled with the spirit of classicism.

My aim here is to bind together, as far as possible, all the various strands in Wendy Taylor's work, and to offer for the first time a complete survey of a prolific and prodigious talent.

CHAPTER ONE

Wendy Taylor was born in Stamford, Lincolnshire. This simple statement, like so many statements of its type, is misleading. In fact her roots are not in a quietly elegant country town but in the East End of London. In Bow, to be precise. Her family belonged to what one might call the "aristocratic" section of the traditional London working class.

Today Wendy Taylor still lives in Bow, and her parents live a few doors away. The remnants of the kind of world she knew as a child are still visible, still within reach. She understands how her neighbours think: their solidarity, their resistance to outsiders, and also their mutual antagonisms. She empathises with what remains of the local culture, and draws on its traditions.

This East End background is one important aspect of Wendy Taylor's character, and of her work. It explains her independence of mind, her inability to take things for granted. Yet her career as a sculptor was shaped by other important factors as well, which have nothing to do with Bow and its inhabitants. For one thing, she is a child of the 1960s, and this was a revolutionary epoch in British art. At the age of sixteen she arrived at St Martin's School of Art. The year was 1961, and she remained there until 1967, teaching part-time at another college during her final year. St Martin's then had the reputation of being the most important training ground for young sculptors in England, and its graduates dominated the New Generation exhibitions at the Whitechapel Art Gallery which set the tone for a complete change in direction in three-dimensional work – a change which involved a shift in attitudes towards colour and form, and also, in many cases, the exploration of new materials, such as transparent plastics and fibreglass.

The British sculptors of the 1960s were very much influenced by one man, Anthony Caro, who taught at St Martin's one day a week, yet dominated the way people thought there. Their work, however, was already distinguishable from Caro's. It had none of the heavy industrial look which Caro had inherited from his American exemplar, David Smith. It was smoother, blander, more minimal without being strictly speaking Minimalist. Caro's work looked both industrial and architectural. That of the New Generation sculptors seemed more closely related to interior design: to shop fittings, and the kind of eye-catchers that architects invent as ornaments for nightclubs. Its strength and its

1. London Dock 1973

8

weakness was that it was very much of its own time. A great deal of it has not in fact lasted very well, either aesthetically or in purely physical terms.

It is possible to see from Wendy Taylor's early work that she was part of this excitement. It is also possible to see that she stood a little apart from it. What rescued her (that is the way it should be put) were two things – family background and gender. The fact that she came from a working-class background meant that she had to take sculpture extremely seriously if she was going to be involved with it at all. There was no money to waste on amateurism. During this period art students in Britain were still largely upper middle-class, but that applied to women much more emphatically than it did to men. In the 1960s working-class males were making a breakthrough in the visual arts; they were also becoming conspicuously successful in related fields, such as fashion photography (David Bailey and Terence Donovan) and design. Art schools did have a complement of female students, but it was still almost automatically assumed that these would come from "good" backgrounds. In fact, part of the dynamic of such schools was a mingling of the classes by way of a mingling of the sexes. As someone who was both working-class and female, Wendy Taylor was an anomaly. It can be assumed that at least some of her tutors, and some of her fellow students, found her presence at St Martin's threatening. This situation may have been personally painful at the time, but it offered freedom from aesthetic shibboleths.

If one looks at the work Wendy Taylor produced from 1966 to 1969 – that is, in her first independently creative period – one does see ideas and combinations of form

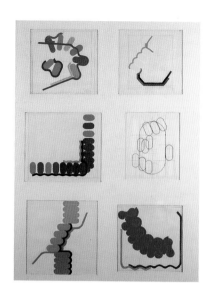

2. Two of a series of mounted drawings 1965-7

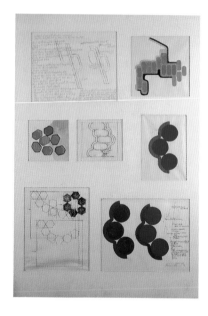

3. Series I 1965

10

which were very much in the idiom of the time. The least personal sculptures, indicatively, are not always the earliest. I say "indicatively" because what one seems to see is a young artist searching through currently available formulae in order to discover what is useful and usable and what is not.

The earliest sculptures which Wendy Taylor thinks of as being fully characteristic – and thus the earliest illustrated in this book – are a group of eight pieces simply called **The Series** (1966). These featured oval or (later) round capsule shapes surrounded, or partly surrounded, by a flange. In one case the capsule is greatly elongated and bent at right angles, so as to create an upright form, but the other pieces cling closely to the ground. In using the capsules, Taylor says that she was "looking for an abstract form that didn't relate to anything specific, either natural or man-made", and also for shapes which would serve as a vehicle for colour. Yet she was, at the same time, influenced by images of natural growth, the forms and

4. Series II 1966

5. Series III 1966

6. Series VI 1966

colours of a garden. The end results do not therefore seem completely abstract. They read instead as abstractions made from plant life. When they were seen out of doors, which is the way in which the sculptor imagined them, problems of scale arise – they are not wholly successful in their relationship to the natural setting."A lesson quickly learned", Taylor now remarks.

Other early sculptures seem to pull in contrary directions. **Blue Spill** (1965-6) is figurative in a coded way. It was inspired by a dripping tap – the silver tube is a regular stream of droplets, the "spill' is the surface spreading out at the bottom. The cluster of blue bubbles at the top – a feature rapidly borrowed by one or two of Taylor's contemporaries – were, she says, an ad hoc solution, a not particularly logical way of finishing the sculpture off. Though **Blue Spill** was on occasion exhibited out of doors, it is in essence an indoor piece by the very nature of its materials. Taylor was soon to grow dissatisfied with the idea of sculpture which seemed to demand a museum setting if it was to have any effect.

Enclave (1969) and **Triad** (1971, but conceived earlier) are a complete contrast to **Blue Spill**. Both were made to be seen out of doors and both are abstract – indeed the workings of geometry are part of their message to the spectator. Under certain conditions, for example, **Enclave** casts a shadow which is a perfect square. **Triad** is made up from the opposite sides of an octahedron, but from a central viewpoint also appears as a square.

At first sight, **Enclave** looks like a simplified, rationalised version of the space-enclosing, ground-devouring sculptures produced by Anthony Caro earlier in the 1960s, and shows one of Caro's typical mannerisms in its rejection of a base. Yet it is very different from his work in important respects. It is, for example, regular and rational, where Caro's conjunctions of form are intuitive. It also invites the spectator into the space occupied by the work (hence the title), rather than warning him or her off a particular patch of territory, which is what Caro's sculptures tend to do. Taylor points to another, not immediately obvious aspect of the work: the fact that it taught her the importance of permanent siting for large sculptures. Disassembling, transporting and reassembling the piece for successive temporary exhibitions was not one of her happier moments.

Two other pieces from the second half of the 1960s, **Daybreak** (1966) and **Deep Glow** (1966) are different again, and now seem to have a much stronger period flavour. Taylor says that the form, which springs from the fact that both are made of wood, is the product of

7. Blue Spill 1965-6

8. Triad 1971

9. Enclave 1969

personal circumstances. After making **Blue Spill** she developed a temporary allergy to fibreglass, and had to work in some other material. Essentially each sculpture consists of an elongated box-section, closed at either end, which is bent and twisted to make a shape, but which remains in the same plane. In the case of **Deep Glow** the box-form is compromised by curves and scallops along its edges. The sculpture is bilaterally symmetrical, and anthropomorphic; it resembles a stylised figure standing on two widely splayed legs.

Daybreak, though superficially similar, is more inventive formally. The box-section or square tube is twisted so as to make a single, asymmetrical calligraphic gesture. The twists and turns are emphasised by the fact that one of the surfaces – what one may think of as the inner or protected one – is painted a deep pink, which contrasts with the blue of the rest of the sculpture. Colour contrasts of this type, and in fact more or less within this range of tones, were very much part of the language of British abstract sculpture in the 1960s. It is the choice of colours, as

13. Gazebo 1969-83 (edition of 5)

11. Untitled maquettes 1967

10. Daybreak 1966

12. Deep Glow 1966

14

well as the springy, aspiring shape of the piece, which justifies the title. Wendy Taylor was to use ribbon-like forms of this type again later.

Gazebo (1969) is also a prophetic work, though a less characteristic one. It is prophetic in the sense that it is an attempt to create a sculptural work which is also a ''place''. As the title implies (gazebo = gaze about) it is intended less as a shelter than as a means of framing a view or series of views. Like **Enclave**, but more directly and emphatically, it invites the spectator to come into the space of the piece, which is admirable for the logic and simplicity with which it solves a particular problem. The structure consists of two large tubes which intersect at right angles, with a circular platform of the same diameter to stand or sit on at the point where they cross. This demonstrates the kind of practical thinking which will reappear in more mature works, applied to increasingly complex situations.

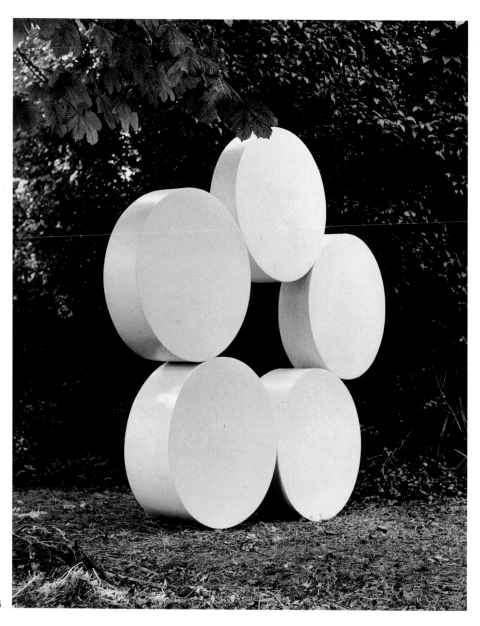

14. Nocturne 1968

16

Gazebo has a Minimalist look, but is not as minimal (because of the need to provide a floor) as some purely sculptural works which Wendy Taylor made at about the same time. **Nocturne** and **Chevron** (both 1968) are concerned with an interplay of geometrical forms – triangle against circle. **Chevron** consists of stacked tubes, arranged in the formation suggested by the title. **Nocturne** is subtler – there are five discs, a bit like the circular capsules found in **The Series**, but with square not rounded edges. Seen from the front, these form a rectangular pentagon, standing upright on one edge.

However, the discs also diminish in thickness the further they get from the base, so, when seen directly from the side, **Nocturne** is pyramidal rather than pentagonal. The "meaning" of the sculpture lies in the interplay between the two views, one form gradually becoming dominant over the other as one moves around the piece.

The idea of discs in regular formation is also basic to the two sculptures which seem to me to be the most original of this period of Wendy Taylor's work, and also the most suggestive and poetic. One is **Calendula** (1966-7), which consists of seven discs of identical size, fixed to a brick wall to make a circular pattern. The point here is not so much the forms themselves, taken in isolation, but the pattern of shadows they cast on the brickwork according to the time of day and the conditions of light. The discs seem to float against their background because they are semicircular in profile – that is, each one is a slice cut from a sphere.

15. Calendula 1967

16. Chevron 1968

Calthae (1967) once again consists of seven discs
arranged to make a circular pattern. The discs are
considerably larger than those used for **Calendula** –
they are five feet six inches in diameter as opposed to
two feet six inches. Made of bright orange fibreglass,
they are designed to float on the surface of a large
stretch of water, each disc being separately anchored
in such a way that the sculpture responds to the
slightest changes in wind and weather. Under the
influence of the wind the discs move, and distort the
pattern, but settle again to make a perfect circle when
the breeze drops and the water calms. The sculpture
both responds to and is a metaphor for nature. Wendy
Taylor says that in order to make ends meet she was
working as a gardener in a public park at the time when
the sculpture was made, and that the orange discs are
the flower heads in a densely planted bed of marigolds
she used to see every day – ''Marigolds'', she adds,
''the first visual impact!'' There is thus a direct link to
the nature-imagery found in the sculptures of **The
Series**, which was in fact made only a year earlier.

17. Calthae 1967

18. Untitled 1967
silk-screen print

During the 1960s Wendy Taylor also made a considerable number of drawings, paintings and prints. Many of the drawings, such as those offered as part of her presentation for the Sainsbury Award (she was one of the joint winners in 1966) relate directly to her sculptures, as might be expected. The paintings employ similar elements too, sometimes arranging them in configurations reminiscent of Kandinsky's work in the 1920s.

Some of the prints, however, break away almost completely from the idiom of the three-dimensional work. A few, such as the silk-screen prints **4/6** (1967) and **As I Walk Through the Trees** (1968), explore the possibilities of apparent movement offered by Op Art. They seem to be influenced by then fashionable artists such as Vasarely and Jesus Raphaël Soto. Others are images printed on Perspex – a medium Wendy Taylor would continue to use during the 1970s. These exploit the effects of depth and shadow this particular medium makes possible (they can thus be related to the sculpture **Calendula** in particular). Good examples of Wendy Taylor's use of Perspex at this time are **Column** and **Square Formation** (both 1969). These mark the beginning of her exploration of the possibilities of abstraction combined with illusionism which was to be continued during the following decade.

19. As I Walk through the Trees
1968 silk-screen print

21. Column 1969 silk-screen on Perspex

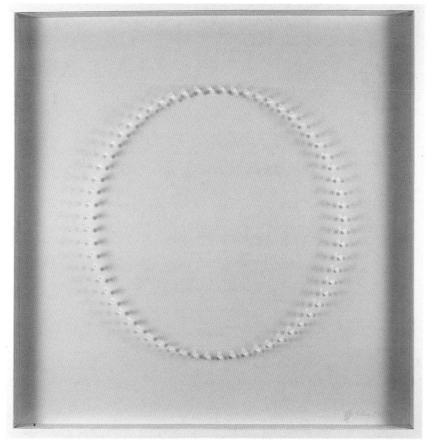

20. Square Formation 1969
silk-screen on Perspex

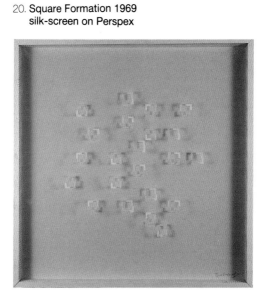

CHAPTER TWO

The years from 1970 to 1972 witnessed a number of major developments in Wendy Taylor's work – in some respects this brief period is the most dramatic in her whole development as an artist. One important event was a request to make a large sculpture for a specific site – a landscaped garden in North London. This sculpture, though not a public commission in the usual sense of the term, introduced her to many of the problems which such commissions were to bring with them later, chief among them the fact that a large sculpture, permanently sited, was something that had to be properly engineered. Called **The Travellers** (1970), it consists of three units placed in a line, each with a sweeping triangular roof. Wendy Taylor says:

> **The Travellers** developed from the sides/walls of the **Gazebo** – the part of that piece I liked the best. I needed height and direction. The garden, though very large and beautiful, had steep banks at either side; it was viewed from the house at first-floor level. Your eye always ended up down by the large cedar tree and the dark corner beyond. I wanted the eye to keep moving round the garden, hence the way the forms rise up. I wanted the work to be part of the garden, not just in it. I wanted it to have an active role as well as working in itself.

> Of course, when I stood back, after completing the work, I realised that, along with the dwarf maples etc., plus the colour, how much like a Japanese gate the work was. In fact, the units look like the entrances to a Shinto shrine. The oriental association is reinforced by the fact that the sculpture is painted the bright scarlet characteristic of some types of lacquer.

The units, however, also look rather nautical. There is something sail-like about the elements I have described as "roofs", and all three units lean at an angle, like a sailing ship heeling in a strong wind. This is an exciting, dynamic piece. Looking at it, one feels some of the excitement the artist herself must have felt when offered the commission, which marked a big step forward in her career. There is a certain irony in the fact that the sculpture has in fact "travelled" further than either artist or patron intended, since it has been moved from the setting it was designed for, and is now in the grounds of a children's hospice in Cambridge.

Despite its importance in career terms, **The Travellers** is not completely representative of Wendy Taylor's sculptural preoccupations at this time.

What the other sculptures made during this period have in common is a growing interest in illusionism. They can

22. The Travellers 1970

23. Floor Piece 1970

24. Elevation 1970

be split into two groups. In one group, the earlier, the illusionistic effects are less flamboyant. **Floor Piece** (1970) is a visual puzzle, of the type beloved by M. C. Escher. It consists of a two-dimensional pattern made of square-section steel tubing, laid flat on the floor. When the design is viewed from the correct angle, the pattern loses its flatness, and rears up to create a three-dimensional structure.

Elevation (1970) offers a simpler form of levitation: a hollow rectangle is mounted on a low base, which supports it on only two of its four sides – the other two are cantilevered. The base is so low and so inconspicuous that the hollow rectangle looks as if it is hovering a few inches above the floor.

Recoil (1970) is still simpler, and the illusionistic element is less emphatic. In fact, there is less a strictly visual contradiction and more a mental one. A metal tube is mounted on a metal block, which supports it for only a small part of its length. Since the support is so small, in relation to the actual projection, it seems as if the sculpture is unstable and must tip over at any moment. The cantilever works for two reasons – the tube is light compared with the supporting block, and one element is pinned to the other. The mind, somehow, finds it hard to absorb these self-evident facts.

25. Recoil 1970

Pursuing this line of thought – heavy materials shown apparently on the point of balance – Wendy Taylor started to feel that the presentation might be oversubtle, only communicating its message to people who already had some kind of visual training. Her studio was then at St Katharine Docks in London where there were lengths of chain lying around, reminders of its nautical past. ''I looked around my own patch of the docks for something that was universally known and taken for granted in its role, and then reversed it.'' The sculptures featuring chains offer a complete contradiction of normal expectations. The main element in **Inversion** (1970), for example, is a simple, highly polished metal beam. This is spanned by two chains fastened, on either side of the beam, to fittings which seem to be bolted to the floor. The beam appears to be tugging at these chains, which are at full stretch in the attempt to stop it rising to the ceiling. But the chains are rigid, not flexible, and they are holding the metal element aloft, not restraining it. **Restrain** (1970) presents a similar, but slightly more complex version of the same situation. In this case there are two beams which rest flat on the floor. Each carries two fasteners,

26. Inversion 1970

24

27. Restrain 1970

duly fitted with chains. These chains, in turn, reach to other fasteners on either side of a third beam of the same size, which floats above the two on the floor and seems to buck and struggle in the effort to get away – it not only levitates but is placed at an angle. Almost automatically, the spectator anthropomorphises the situation – this third beam is endowed with will and personality; it becomes, for instance, a bucking, tethered horse.

The illusionistic element in these sculptures, and others like them, is extraordinarily strong. "I am always amazed", Wendy Taylor says, "particularly by architects and even engineers, believe it or not, who come out with the most extraordinary remarks on how it is done. Anything from magnets to helium! It only goes to show how many people have a fixed idea of what chain is and what it can do. I have had some quite heated arguments with people who have stood in front

28. Artist working in the forge at Gate 24 c. 1973

29. Maquette for Transom 1973

30. Inspan 1971

of one of the chain pieces and told me 'it's impossible' when actually looking at it." She adds: "For me it's all about not taking things for granted without wondering about them – gravity, materials, etc. – plus about using forms which are in appearance heavy and making them light ... Another side is humour: I've come to accept and enjoy this and now enjoy others' pleasure in it."

It must be said that not everyone in the British art world was amused when these sculptures first appeared. For one thing, they offered a strong challenge to the then fashionable doctrine of "factuality". In this case, what you saw was by no means what you got. Minimal elements were used (the metal beams could be regarded as a Minimalist commonplace), but this aspect was subverted by the way in which the forms were presented. Pompous people did not care for this – they suspected the joke might be at their own expense. Quite apart from that, many of the artist's contemporaries felt challenged, and abashed, by the meticulous craftsmanship, which was integral to the effect made by the sculptures – the exquisite precision of handling was what made the illusion viable. Wendy Taylor notes ruefully that she had "a lot of early studio disasters" when making the pieces because the welding needed was so difficult. In spite of the fact that the sculptures had been inspired by "found" chain discovered lying around in the docks, such found material could rarely be used for the finished artwork – Taylor had to buy links which were the exact proportion required. Even this small detail shows how finely everything to do with the sculptures was calculated.

31. Rigging 1975 drawing

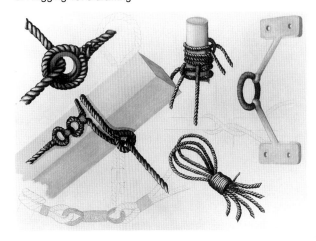

Early items in the **Chain** series, which has continued to grow and develop, included, in addition to the two sculptures already described, **Liberation** (1970), where a single beam rears up skywards, restrained by two chains. The proportions are curiously reminiscent of the crouching marble lions made in ancient Greece – those still on Delos, for instance. There is also **Inspan** (1971), where a steel tube like the one which forms part of **Recoil** is wrapped in a restraining chain. This makes the connection between the chain pieces and the sculptures which immediately preceded them very clear. During this period there were also two sculptures made from chain alone, **Suspension** and **Sky Hook** (both 1972). The idea here is somewhat different from that found in the main group. The chain becomes an independent entity – a loop in one case, a kind of cradle in the other – hanging from something invisible. To my mind, the illusionistic effect is much less compelling – one immediately sees that the chain is in fact rigid, a self-sustaining structure.

During this time Wendy Taylor also made a great deal of graphic work. Some examples – her Perspex prints – looked back to **Enclave** where the play of shadow is as important as the actual forms. Others were drawings related to the chain pieces, some directly, like a drawing for **Liberation** (1970), which shows the piece more or less as it was made, apart from a difference in the angle of the beam. Other drawings explore ideas which were not used, and others still are studies of possibly useful details, or even of detritus from the docks which fell into the same category of ''found'' material as the chains (**Anchor and Pipes**, 1971). All these drawings demonstrate the very high quality of Wendy Taylor's draughtsmanship – they are extremely assured, and the handling is always refined. They are, and this is a paradox, extremely realistic drawings of forms which might be considered abstract in many cases – the confusion between ''real'' and ''not real'' is complete, especially when we consider that many represent what might be considered physical impossibilities.

The taste for illusionistic representation also emerges strongly in a group of montages produced at this time which make up a rather isolated episode in Wendy Taylor's development as an artist. These record details and close-ups of ruined buildings in a rather surreal way, and seem to have been inspired by the demolition Wendy Taylor saw going on all around her in Docklands, where her studio now was, and in the East End. One significant feature of these montages is the fact that they show a fascination with brickwork. This aspect of the montages does look forward to some future developments in Wendy Taylor's work.

32. Drawing for Liberation 1970

33. Sky Hook 1972

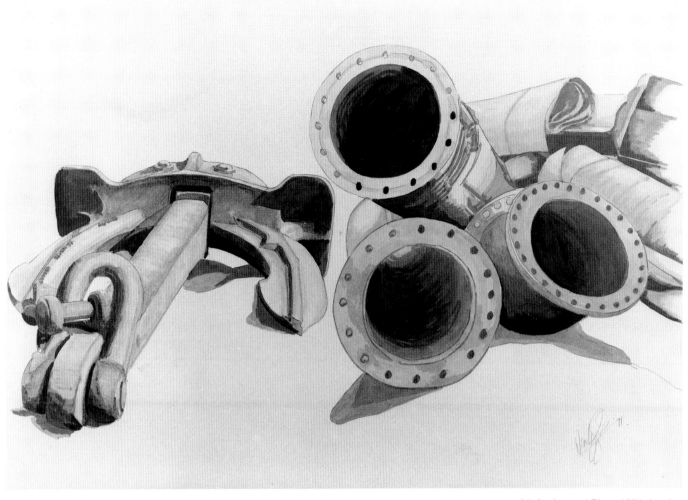

34. Anchor and Pipes 1971 drawing

35. Wire Rope 1975 drawing

36. Suspension maquette 1972

CHAPTER THREE

The period 1973 to 1976 saw Wendy Taylor starting to establish a public presence for her work. It was also the period during which she exhibited most frequently in commercial galleries. Of her nine solo exhibitions to date, five took place between 1974 and 1976. To some extent, therefore, many of the works made in the early and middle 1970s reflect Taylor's increasingly reluctant involvement with the mechanisms of the commercial art world. She continued to develop the **Chain** series, finding new and ingenious variations on an established theme. Some of these sculptures, in addition to being made full-scale, were offered as maquettes, sometimes in editions.

One feature of these later **Chain** sculptures is the effort to explore the possibilities offered by an enclosed space – a room or gallery. **Trail** and **Transom** (both 1973) are tubes wrapped or looped in chain. Both cling closely to the floor. **Transom** is particularly successful in conveying the idea that the tube is levitating rather than being supported. The chain no longer "restrains". It now hangs limply around the tube which accepts its presence, so to speak, rather than fighting against it.

There continue to be allusions to earlier work. In **Square Piece** (maquette 1973) the metal frame seen in **Elevation** is made to stand vertically, and trails a loop of chain from its lowest element, which is parallel to the floor. **Oblique** (two maquettes, 1976 and 1977) takes this concept further. The main form is now a solid metal square, a shallow enclosed box. This metal square is tilted obliquely, and has a piece of chain rather casually draped over it which it is dragging upwards. The thing which fascinates the spectator here is the fact that the sculpture looks completely off balance. Even if one has worked out the fact that the chain is rigid, not flexible, and that it is the supporting element, not a laxly dependent one, there still seems no logical reason for the piece to remain in an upright position – that is, unless the square is actually levitating after all.

The same effect is used in **Poise** (1975) where a vertical tube, floating in the air, dangles a loop of chain which reaches the floor. The vertical element is so far removed from the centre of the loop, which would appear to be also the centre of gravity, that one cannot see why the sculpture remains stable – as quite clearly it does.

A scale model made to show how the various works included were going to be positioned, part of Wendy Taylor's preparations for her show held at the Oliver

37. Poise 1975

Dowling Gallery, Dublin, in 1976, shows how carefully all these effects were worked out, not only in themselves, but in relation to the space available. One thing which the model also demonstrates, mutedly but perhaps in some ways more eloquently than words, is the desire for a kind of control which the artist is nearly always denied by the commercial gallery system, however cordial the personal relationships may be.

Between 1973 and 1976 Wendy Taylor made two important public sculptures, very different from one another and based on different ideas of what public art was or might be. One was in the end an extremely successful and fruitful experience, the other was a disaster.

Timepiece (1973) was born in special circumstances. Some of these were extremely personal, a mixture of irritation and the competitive spirit. Wendy Taylor recalls the situation thus:

> There was a great project about, something to do with the Peter Stuyvesant Foundation – I can't remember the details now, but something like "six sculptors in six cities". Anyway, the scheme was that a number of artists would be asked to make a piece of large outdoor sculpture (lump sum provided in advance) for a particular city. Once the work was made it would be exhibited for six months (I think). At the end of that period the city concerned would either buy the work, or it would be returned to the artist. I had genuinely hoped, because of my clear preoccupation with this field, to be at least short-listed. I wasn't, and I was really fed up – feeling desperately low and rejected. Yet, while all this was gnawing away, I also realised (it started as a kind of consolation) that the works commissioned had no guarantee of being permanent. In addition, London was not on the list of cities. So I decided to make a maquette of what I would do if given the chance, with a view to the sculpture being both permanent and in London.

39. One-man show at the Oliver Dowling Gallery, Dublin 1976

40. Model of gallery installation to show exact position of works 1976

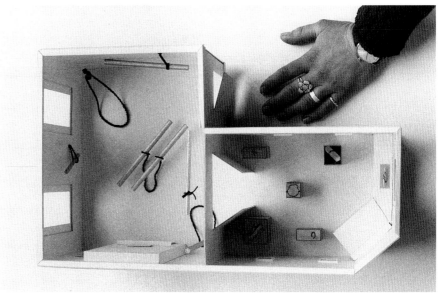

32

41. Oblique maquette 1976-7

At this time Wendy Taylor was occupying a studio in St Katharine Docks (one of several spaces she successively had there). The Tower Hotel was in course of construction nearby and she chose this as the ''fantasy'' location for her proposed London sculpture. The choice was made not merely because of the site's propinquity, but because of actual family connections with the area:

> I wanted to make a piece that was a tribute and a celebration of the amazing concept the docks represented – their construction, use and operation.

What she came up with was the idea of a large sundial, which would also be unmistakably a work of contemporary sculpture. There were a number of reasons, some internal (to do with her own development as an artist), some external (to do with the site she coveted). For example, she had already made a number of pieces where the shadows cast played almost as important a part as the actual structure – **Enclave** was one example which seemed relevant when she was thinking about the project. The local associations were with navigation – and navigation is to do with real time, not with mean time. The fact that Greenwich, which sets mean time, was so close seemed to sharpen the contrast between the two conceptions of time rather than blurring it.

42. Installing Timepiece at St Katharine Docks 1973

43. Timepiece 1973

44. Detail of Timepiece 1973

Having decided on a sundial, she chose to use actual forms which she saw around her in the docklands as its components – that is, in addition to the chains she had already used:

> The "ring" of the sundial is in fact a large washer; the gnomon or pointer is a huge enlargement of the traditional dockyard nail. I used shackles for the sides, and chains for the supports. With this particular sundial, the sun, in summer, casts a shadow on the face; when the sun is low in the sky it casts a shadow on the inner ring.

Getting from the maquette to the full-scale work was a matter of good luck and good will:

> Because the people on the site used to call into the studio, mainly out of curiosity, they got to know what I was up to. What I was doing was somehow brought to the attention of the owners of the hotel, which was then part of the J. Lyons Group. I was introduced to one of them at the Globe Theatre site where I was exhibiting. To my amazement he had already heard of my maquette and asked to see photographs. I thought he was just being polite, and did not send them – I didn't own a camera and thought, in any case, that they would simply end up in the wastepaper basket. He repeated this request in writing, so I sent the pictures. Almost by return of post he asked me to proceed.

Timepiece gave Wendy Taylor the two things she probably needed most at this time – on the one hand, visibility and identity as someone who made public sculpture; on the other, essential practical experience in creating work of this type: how to engineer this piece, how to make sure it would be safe and durable, and how to manage the necessary collaborations involved (with professional engineers on the one hand, and with industrial fabricators on the other). As I have noted in my preface, **Timepiece** soon became one of the symbols of contemporary London, almost taken for granted as much as its neighbour, Tower Bridge.

The story of **Havering Unit** (1973) is less happy. The 1970s saw an effort to find social functions of new kinds for contemporary art. Wendy Taylor got drawn into this movement when she was commissioned by the Teachers' Advisory Centre to design a three-dimensional object for a school playground. Various parts of her previous experience seemed to feed into this task:

> I had worked for quite a long while with an organisation that minded the children of local families while their parents worked. I also spent one summer working in Cable Street with children of "mixed ability" – some very bright, some with behavioural problems, all mixed up with local school children. It was rough, but I had the immense advantage of being local and understanding the language. I took it on when I first left college and was only teaching one and a half days a week – I felt I couldn't just go on the

45. Timepiece construction 1973

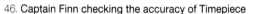

46. Captain Finn checking the accuracy of Timepiece

dole as fellow lecturers did. It left a mountain of different emotions – happy, tragic, wicked. There were stories which, if I hadn't experienced them first-hand, I'd find it hard to believe. This supplied a personal reason for taking the project on.

Another reason was that some of her actual practical experience as a sculptor seemed to lead towards something of this kind. She had, for example, learned the principles of plastic cocooning through making **Chevron**. This cocooning was originally used to protect the Princess flying boats which were developed during the war and moored at Southampton, and was later used extensively for ships and submarines, as well as for heavy machinery in transit. Taylor now thought that the process might be applied to covering shapes made from foam rubber, soft enough for children to play with safely. She developed a kit of twenty-five shapes which could be arranged in various ways. These were demonstrated at the City of London Polytechnic, then tested on a television programme about play furniture made by Pebble Mill at One.

The kit of shapes seemed to be a great success. Children liked and responded well to them. Inundated with orders after the television transmission, Taylor started to envisage a future where the kit would supply the income which would enable her to continue her career as an artist without constant financial strain.

47. Havering Unit 1973 litho prints

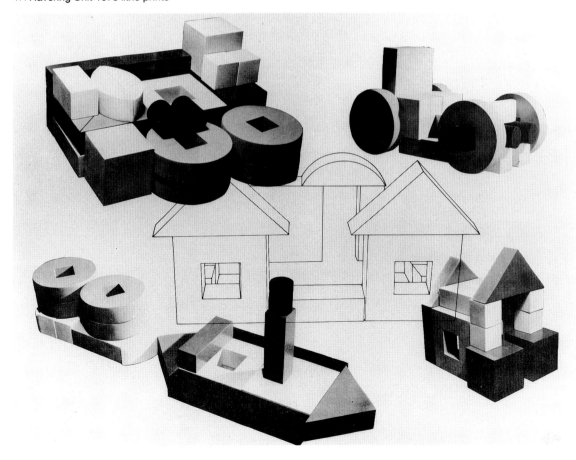

The unit was now delivered to the school in Havering for which it had originally been designed. The school used it for several months, and troubles began to appear. During very cold weather the surface became brittle. The reason was that the coating was not up to the specification of the original samples. The contractors admitted liability and remade the unit. Unfortunately the second version was completely substandard, as now the coating was not to the thickness required.

Wendy Taylor sued those responsible – and won. It was, as she now says, "several years of misery". By the time the suit was settled, the rise in petroleum prices (the coating material was made of vinyl chloride copolymer resin, a petroleum product) had put the price out of reach of the local authorities for whom **Havering Unit** was designed.

The story is a little like that of the ill-fated venture made by the great Latin American Constructivist Joaquín Torres-Garcia into making children's toys which were sets of wooden shapes from which more complex forms could be made. He too was frustrated at every turn, and never succeeded in getting a brilliant idea off the ground. The comparison is relevant in more than one respect, as it also points to a strongly Constructivist element in Wendy Taylor's work. She herself says resignedly:

> I personally keep the **Havering Unit** and photos in my records because it was a huge amount of hard work and energy spent in total, and a hard lesson to learn. The project was marred by my lack of experience and money. I wasn't able to handle the bad deal I found myself in.

48. Havering Unit 1973

CHAPTER FOUR

The next phase of Wendy Taylor's work is associated, not with chains and other material associated with the dockyard, but with bricks, real and simulated. However, since artists' careers are seldom as tidy and focused as art historians would like to make them, the later 1970s were not as wholly concerned with a single theme as this thumbnail description might suggest.

Pieces from the **Chain** series were still being produced in the second half of the decade. An example is **Veer** (maquette 1977), which is a version of **Oblique**, now using an oblong box instead of a square, flat-sided one. In the light of hindsight one can perhaps sense that the artist's interest in this particular concept – the chain which supports while seeming to constrain – was beginning to cool.

One reaction was to make sculpture on more classically Modernist lines. A maquette for a different, much simpler and more austere sundial, **Equatorial Sundial** (1977) reveals Taylor's interest in Constructivism quite clearly, and this is still more obvious in a major public sculpture made at this time – **Octo** (1979), commissioned for Milton Keynes. **Octo** had actually been in progress throughout the epoch of the **Chain** pieces. The first maquette dates from 1972 and the full-scale working model from 1973.

It can be related to another maquette, **Sail** (1972), which was never made full-size. This consists of a box-section of metal, which itself forms a hollow square. The sides of the square, which stands upright on one of its corners, twist and undulate in such a way that the sculpture alters its aspect radically, just as **Octo** does, as the spectator progresses round it.

The ideas expressed in **Sail** and **Octo** are also present, though somewhat modified, in the maquette **Balance** (1977-8). What this shares with the two sculptures just mentioned is the idea of shapes resting on what is no more than a point, so that they seem to be inherently unstable; and also the idea of simple forms which transform themselves as the spectator moves, simply because of the way in which they are presented and positioned.

To understand the progress of Taylor's work, and its underlying sensibility, one also has to know something about the setting in which it was made. This continued to be urban. British Modernists, and especially sculptors, have always tended to move out of London as soon as they achieved any degree of success. The

49. Sail maquette 1972-4

reasons are understandable – more space, more tranquillity in which to work, lower living costs, more pleasant surroundings. Henry Moore set the example when he moved to Much Hadham in Hertfordshire in 1940 after his studio in Hampstead was damaged by bombing. The sculptors of the immediately postwar generation, such as Lynn Chadwick and Elisabeth Frink, followed his example. For a while, Frink was to leave England altogether.

Wendy Taylor, on the other hand, remained rooted in the East End of London, where she had been brought up. One suspects that this was not simply due to lack of means, though she remained poor. She gives an eloquent description of her studio and its surroundings, after she was forced to leave St Katharine Docks:

> After a brief period in Stepney I moved to Gate 24, Wapping High Street, several hundred yards down the road from St Katharine. It had been Harland and Wolff's dock workshop. It consisted of a third of an acre, mostly trees. There was a big old forge with over a hundred windows, most of them broken, and a series of sheds with little or nothing in the way of roofs. I think my landlords – the Port of London Authority (there were to be several other landlords later) – found me useful as a kind of security outpost. I worked there weekends as well as some evenings; part-time teaching ate into my weekdays. If there was a fire or strange loud noises, I would go to investigate.
>
> I got to know every corner of those docks. The whole contents of my studio – cupboards, tables, stools, trolleys – came from my foragings. Mum and Dad used to come

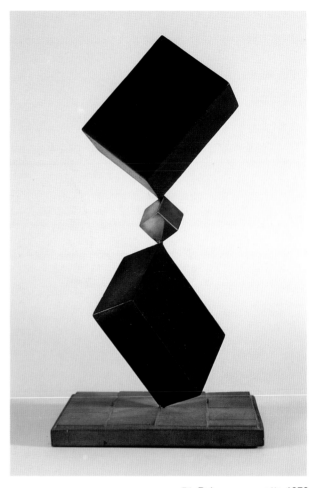

51. Balance maquette 1978

52. Veer maquette 1977

42

53. Artist moving plants from area designated for excavation c. 1973

54. London Dock c. 1973

quite often on a Sunday afternoon with a picnic, and I would take them exploring. I think we could have run a good totter's yard! Some areas were beginning to get quite jungle-like, sprouting ferns and wild flowers. Balsam popped up and had a heady smell; its quite spectacular orchid-like flowers flourished inside a large shed whose roof had gone. Some offices, apart from both live and dead pigeons, were still intact, and gave one a strange *Marie Celeste*-like feeling, with old ledgers still on the desks.

The materials already available were sometimes added to. Fly-tipping occurred from time to time. One lot of rubbish, reputed to be the interior of Danny La Rue's nightclub, stripped out because of a rat infestation, provided me with a marvellous supply of timber. The inner skeleton of the full-size wooden version of **Octo** came from this source; so did quite a bit of the formwork for **Brick Knot**. I used to phone home and say "Can you give us a hand this Sunday, to get a bit more Danny La Rue in?"

Of course conditions were not always as idyllic as this description suggests. There were constant break-ins, mostly by children. There were raiders who came to strip lead from the roofs. There was a rat infestation when a neighbouring sugar warehouse burned down – the rats ate the electric wiring. Yet there was a neighbourliness even about one of these creatures:

I had one rat for years – I used to call him 'Four O'Clock Ratty'. He had a smart white shirt-front and always appeared at four in the afternoon. He was a loner, and unlike the invasion which happened later, he was well-behaved.

One of the things which helped to crystallise the idea for the **Brick** pieces was all the demolition and construction that Wendy Taylor saw around her at this time. Yet there were other, more specific experiences as well:

At weekends I used to go with a friend who was an architect to visit some of his sites. I was fascinated by the brick sample panels – we spent ages looking at them and comparing them. They showed different colours of brick, different mortar joints and mortar colour, and so forth. These samples were known as "tombstones" and in brick factories they occupied what is known as the "graveyard". They were all about three to four feet high, and were grouped together for comparison.

Another important experience came during a trip abroad which allowed time to digest these images. Wendy Taylor's then dealer was showing her work at the Bologna Art Fair, and she drove there with a friend who also had some work to do in Venice:

Looking out of the car I saw all those tall chimney stacks in the industrial area just before you get to Venice itself. Looking at them, I suddenly realised what I wanted to do.

Because its purchase by the Tate Gallery generated a major journalistic scandal, the best known piece of sculpture made of brick, in England at least, is **Equivalent VIII** (1965), by the American Minimal artist Carl Andre. **Equivalent VIII** is everything which Wendy Taylor's **Brick** sculptures are not. It is literal, anti-illusionistic and made of discrete units (it can all be taken apart, brick by brick, then – if required – put back together again according to the prescribed pattern). Even though it is so "literal", its true existence is really as a diagram which exists or existed in the artist's head. The bricks are merely convenient units, not especially meaningful in themselves, but a means of making the diagram fully visible to the audience. Paradoxically, in Taylor's **Brick** series the bricks themselves matter more than they do in Andre's work.

Brick Knot, the earliest of the sculptures, is, like the pieces in the **Chain** series, concerned with paradox and illusion. It consists of a strip or ribbon, apparently made of bricks, bent back on itself and tied (as the title suggests) into a knot. The first maquette for the sculpture dates from 1976; the full-sized version dates from 1977-8. As with the **Chain** series, our first reaction to the sculpture is apt to be disbelief. Bricks are rectilinear objects which, as in the ordinary brick wall, are commonly used to make equally rectilinear forms.

55. Brick Knot 1977-8

56. Detail of Counterpoise 1979-80

In actual fact, the bricks we see in this case are a simulacrum – the sculpture is made of fibreglass:

> I had to spend ages trying to find a way of making brick slips out of another, lighter material because I couldn't see how I could manage the weight of the real thing, working alone in the studio. I used all the ingredients of brick – sawdust, ground-fired kiln plaster instead of clay, iron filings, etc., bonded together with resin and pigmented so as to try and get the same variation one gets in fired brick.

The illusion was so successful that Taylor soon went on to make other sculptures based on the same theme. The range of variation is much wider than that found in the **Chain** series.

Some of these variations are, like **Brick Knot**, essentially abstract forms, whose abstraction is (so to speak) contradicted by the presence of the bricks themselves, the most mundane of recognisable objects. This is the case with **Crossbow** (maquette 1977, full-scale version 1978), where a square expanse of brickwork seems to bend in response to being compressed by a loop of rope joining opposing corners. It is also the case with **Counterpoise** (1979-80), except that the sculpture here is made of real bricks bonded to a reinforced concrete core – an astonishing technical feat. This coiled strip of brickwork takes the fiction of the two earlier pieces and transforms it into something almost as literal as the Carl Andre. Here, too, the compression of the basic units is a large part of the message, just as elements in tension is the message of the **Chain** series.

In these three sculptures the Constructivist influence remains strong. **Brick Knot** and **Counterpoise**, with their twisted, ribbon-like shapes, are related to **Octo** (which will be discussed in more detail in a moment), and all three works have a close kinship to the work of Max Bill, with its dependence on mathematical formulae to produce a kind of harmony in sculpture which would be accessible to the intellect as well as to purely visceral and intuitive reactions.

Other sculptures featuring bricks seem to explore concerns which are entirely different. Some are maquettes for sculptural installations, made to fit a particular gallery space, in preparation for a proposed one-person show. There is a claustrophobic **Brick Maze** (1977) for example, and another model which shows the same space almost entirely filled by two gargantuan interlocking brick frames. These, even if unconsciously, comment on the constraints imposed by the gallery situation itself.

There are also sculptures and maquettes where Taylor's concern with architecture is more directly expressed. One maquette shows a section of roof supported on a single brick pillar; another is a model of a brick section made of brick and wood. There were American artists who made similar works a little later, in the 1980s – a cross between sculptures and architectural models. (The inspiration seemed to come from the architectural miniatures which have long been produced in the workshops attached to the great Hollywood film studios.) The piece in this category which Taylor took the furthest is **Brick Arch** (1978). This introduces yet another variation on the theme of illusionism. The arch consists of two mismatched pillars, set at an angle to one another and spanned by a grid-like structure in the shape of an arch. That is, the bricks themselves are absent here, and metal has been used to represent the mortar which would, or should, bind them together. The twist created by misaligning the pillars deliberately confuses the message. The sculpture asks interesting questions about the way in which we read what we see: is pattern more important than material? Here the insistent, familiar pattern is present, but the material is absent, though the supporting pillars tell us what it ought to be.

Finally, there is a group of small works – nominally maquettes – where everyday objects are turned into brickwork. A very similar trick is played in some of Magritte's paintings, but in two dimensions not in three. The maquettes in this group include a still life with a bottle and apples, a carton with six eggs in it, and a fruit stand piled with fruit. The forms have been subtly altered to give them a certain blunt quality, appropriate to things made of brick. They are fractionally simplified, so as to respond to the supposedly coarse nature of the material. Taylor says that the bluntness of style was also a reaction to teaching student drawing-classes – to the slight stiffness and involuntary simplification found in many drawings of still-life subjects.

57. Untitled
(Bridge section)
1978

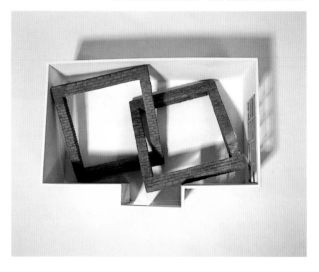
58. Untitled
(Roof section)
1978

59. Link installation 1:20 scale model 1977

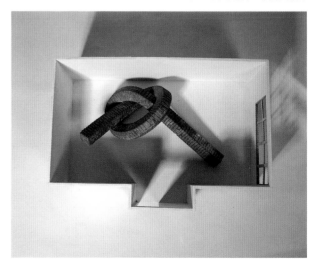

60. Brick Maze installation 1:20 scale model 1977

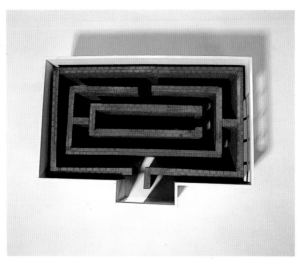

61. Knot Installation 1:20 scale model 1977

62. Eggs 1979

63. Fruit Stand 1979

64. Still Life 1979

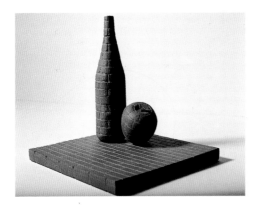

65. Crossbow 1977-8

architects and – looking now in a very different direction – she has to communicate efficiently with engineers and fabricators, the people who will help her to get the sculpture made.

Wendy Taylor's sculptures embody, and also typify, a subtle shift in studio practice which has taken place during the past quarter of a century. One can see what this shift is by looking very briefly at the history of British Modernist sculpture in the twentieth century. The Modernism of the period between the two World Wars had in fact involved an unexpected leap backwards into the handcrafted and handmade. This involved not only Eric Gill, who in any case had his roots in the Arts and Crafts Movement of the nineteenth century, but also Jacob Epstein and Henry Moore. Epstein had two very different approaches to technique. Some major sculptures were carved directly from the block by the artist himself, in the manner of Michelangelo. Others, notably his numerous portraits, were multiples cast in bronze, in numbered editions. For these he needed the collaboration of a foundry. The procedure he followed conformed to a pattern established in European art in the eighteenth and nineteenth centuries.

After World War II, Moore's attitude altered. He could not produce the large volume of work now required of him without the help of studio assistants. He also needed the help not only of a foundry but of the professional marble carvers who still exist in Italy, in and around Carrara. His way of organising his studio therefore reverted to the nineteenth-century pattern. By this time, however, he was so famous that the huge monumental sculptures now commissioned from him seldom had to carry a specific message. What those who commissioned them wanted was a recognisable Henry Moore. Inflexible in content, they were also conservative in technique, being made of marble or bronze, the traditional materials for public sculptures since ancient Greece and Rome.

Wendy Taylor was not in this kind of situation. Her clients often wanted a work which would carry a specific message, particular to their own situation. The materials used were often unconventional, or else were traditional materials employed in unexpected ways. Finding a solution was a matter of dialogue with the artist. When the solution to a particular problem had been identified, then the work itself had to be built. If it was to be in a public spot, and accessible to the public, as was usually the case, then questions of durability and safety arose. There were liberating aspects too. Wendy Taylor says that it was an enormous relief to be able to work on sculptures which did not have to be portable, and where questions of balance and stability were not so crucial, since they could be fixed firmly to the ground.

71. Detail of Essence 1982

72. Transporting Sentinel 1981

To solve the problems that confronted her she needed help, but not necessarily that of artists younger and less experienced than herself – the traditional recourse of successful sculptors from the Renaissance onwards, and the solution adopted by Moore at Much Hadham. What she needed were specialists – engineers who could tell her about the characteristics of the materials she was using, and what stresses they would take – and also fabricators and manufacturers of specific items. No school of art offered training for the multiple roles she was now forced to assume. It was very much a question of learning on and through the job, with each major commission presenting a different set of problems, yet at the same time leaving a residue of knowledge behind it which could be utilised again.

Sentinel (1980-1), the first of the series of public sculptures described in this chapter, is obviously closely related to **Counterpoise** in style, materials and technique. Like the latter, it is made of bricks attached to a reinforced concrete core. Unlike **Brick Knot** or **Counterpoise**, however, it is distinctly anthropomorphic – it can be referred directly to **Deep Glow**, made fourteen years earlier. Like **Deep Glow** it seems to be an abstraction from a figure standing with widespread legs. The knot (in fact a cow-hitch) which joins the "legs" – two brick-clad pillars inclined forward and towards one another – can be read as arms locked behind the figure's head, almost in a classic body builder pose. A slightly different, and to my mind much more fascinating reading, possible when the sculpture is seen obliquely from the front and below, suggests that the figure is carrying a burden. It looks like photographs I have seen of men carrying coracles (primitive wicker and skin boats, still sometimes used in Wales and Ireland) on their backs. Wendy Taylor points to a technical aspect – that the forms are possible only because the sculpture is securely fastened to the ground – it has no inherent stability.

Compass Bowl (1980) can obviously be referred to **Timepiece**, but has less immediate precedent in Wendy Taylor's work than **Sentinel**, which belongs to a whole family of sculptures made, or seeming to be made, of bricks.

The genesis of the commission was characteristically complicated. Through working on **Counterpoise** with its reinforced concrete core, Wendy Taylor had become known to the Cement and Concrete Association. This association put the authorities at Basildon Development Corporation in touch with her, after the latter had been let down by someone else who was supposed to produce an ornamental work in concrete for them.

> My first reaction was to be rather offended, but I agreed to go and look at the site. It was in fact a huge deep muddy hole in the ground. I said, perhaps rather rudely, that I loathed the type of work they seemed to have in mind, but would like to have a go at presenting some of my own ideas. When I was down in the hole I had absolutely no idea of where I was, and I thought other people might have the same feeling of disorientation, so (because the shape was circular) I came up with the idea of a compass. The whole thing would then be a place in its own right, an environment, not just a ventilation hole between two underpasses. I further suggested that the planting should be related both to the walls, and the notion of direction – plants that favoured heat and light on the south, those which liked shade and cool on the north. The Chief Engineer and his colleagues were very impressed by the proposal, even though what I suggested wasn't at all what they had originally envisaged, and they gave me the go-ahead.

There are a number of points to be made here. One is that Wendy Taylor had long been an enthusiastic gardener, and had in fact worked part-time as a gardener in public parks (the genesis of **Calthae**). For the first time her sculptural preoccupations could be extended into actual landscaping. **Compass Bowl** was

74. Sentinel 1980-1

73. **Detail of Sentinel**

75. Southernhay site Basildon 1979

76. Compass Bowl 1:100 scale model 1980

77. Compass Bowl 1980

well liked by the public and in this very specific sense –
perhaps the best sense of all – has proven to be an
enduring success. It was the beginning of a fruitful
association with the authorities in Basildon.

Wendy Taylor's next public commission, **Equatorial
Sundial** (1981-2) for Telephone Rentals plc, has already
been discussed briefly, in connection with the maquette
which dates from 1977. Like **Octo**, the full-scale
sculpture was executed in stainless steel, and is
impressive for its clean lines and economy of form.

Canterbury Relief (1981), like **Compass Bowl**, was a
new departure – a work tailored to fit a very particular
set of circumstances. It was a commission from the
building firm of Wiltshiers, as a memorial to their
founder, Eric Wiltshier, who had died in 1961. The site
was the new council offices in Canterbury which the firm
were just completing:

78. Detail of Equatorial Sundial 1981-2

> Eric Wiltshier was very proud of his roots in Canterbury,
> and also loved the surrounding countryside deeply. His
> firm worked extensively in the Canterbury region,
> especially at its beginnings, though it had now developed
> into an international organisation. I chose – and it turned
> out to be a massive undertaking – to make a relief map of
> the whole of the Canterbury district. This was appropriate,
> not only because Mr Wiltshier had known and loved the
> area so well, but because of the actual site: the council
> offices dealt with housing, planning etc. I wanted the map
> to be absolutely accurate, so that it could be "used" –
> and also so that, in the future, it would serve as a record of
> what actually existed at the time when it was made –
> houses, orchards, and so forth. Many trips were made to
> check. My studio assistant Mark Laidler and I went on
> many journeys armed with a list of queries. It was

79. Equatorial Sundial 1981-2

80. Section showing development of work on Canterbury Relief 1981

81. Canterbury Relief 1981

incredibly exciting to discover that some "mystery" hill was in fact just as one had modelled it in the studio.

For the unveiling I made a small exhibition of photographs showing the work in progress. When I went back to take it down some weeks later I found a council official standing in front of the work explaining to a family who were about to be rehoused exactly where the particular row of houses they were going to was, and what the surroundings were.

Wendy Taylor adds that the project taught her important lessons about the shape of her own career:

I became conscious that it was preferable to exercise my own inventive skills in the studio, observing and then creating, than to teach in colleges, dealing with what seemed to be increasingly indifferent groups of students.

From a technical point of view, the piece was complex. It was in fact the largest "whole" casting undertaken by the foundry which made it – most such work is cast in sections, then welded together later. After the necessary preliminary research had been done, the relief was made to a horizontal scale of one to 10,000 (approximately six inches to the mile). The vertical scale, however, was exaggerated by a factor of eight, so as to make the map easier to read in detail. The relief was built up on a plywood base, reinforced by a metal framework to prevent distortion. Layers of plywood and hardboard, shaped to correspond with the contour lines, were placed in position and the ground was built up over the contour layers using papier-mâché, foam and wooden blocks. The whole was covered in a thin resin and tissue coating, using several layers, and the final contours were checked to see that there had been no distortion due to shrinkage. The construction was then painted, and plotted with pen and ink to show roads, houses, wooded areas, fen and marsh, rivers, lakes, major buildings like churches, and all the orchards which are characteristic of the area:

I had already decided that I wanted the roads to appear as strips of raised, polished bronze, and, to achieve this in the casting, they were cut from black rubber sheet, with sloping sides to prevent undercuts. The material was flexible enough to accommodate the horizontal and vertical bends imposed by the contours. These rubber strips were glued into position and filled so as to cover the joints.

Wooded areas were applied with a spatula, using a mixture of sand, fine wood shavings and textured paint, and rivers and marshes were gouged out. How to show orchards was another problem. It was solved using the rubber normally employed to cover table tennis bats. This proved to be ideal in scale and had the right degree of uniformity to indicate a planned layout.

After it had been completed in this form, the relief was moved to the foundry to be cast. This process was not without its misadventures – Wendy Taylor remembers a crisis when Canterbury cathedral and its immediate surroundings in the very centre of the relief went missing and had to be redone. She now says:

> I don't regard the work as sculpture as such, but as an exercise in tight discipline combined with a multitude of technical challenges.

After making **Canterbury Relief**, Wendy Taylor returned to making sculptures which were more central to her own aesthetic interests. "Central" is a good adjective in more than one respect, for **Essence** (1982) is in fact the core around which **Counterpoise** was built – Wendy Taylor had always intended to make a separate sculpture in a different material. The piece, which was already in reinforced fibreglass, was commissioned by the Milton Keynes Development Corporation as a direct result of the success of **Octo**, and cast in bronze.

Essence and its direct successor **Opus** (1982-3) are entirely abstract works. Yet a critic is always unwise to assume that, just because a work is abstract, the impulse for making it must also be entirely cerebral. Throughout this period, she retained her fascination with nature and natural forms. This is the personal element in the painstakingly accurate **Canterbury Relief**. **Shell Form** (1982), a maquette for a sculpture to be made in marble, shows how Taylor's preoccupation with twisted, ribbon-like shapes, wound around interior voids, could be referred back to a specific source in nature.

83. Essence 1982

82. Essence 1982

The origins of **Opus** are less easy to detect, but in fact this too is rooted in natural forms. Wendy Taylor had always enjoyed drawing animals, and at this time (also earlier and later) worked frequently at London Zoo. A meticulously naturalistic series of drawings devoted to the white rhino was in progress at the same time as she was working on the sculpture – in her own mind there is now a clear connection between the two projects.

One of the things which especially fascinated her about the rhino was the relationship between its bone structure and its heavy skin. This fascination is visible in a drawing of a rhino seen from the rear, lying down. It becomes a series of assymetrical lumps and hollows. Comparing this drawing to **Opus**, one can detect a somewhat similar rhythm of forms.

There is another point of resemblance, perhaps accidental, between the sculpture and these drawings – or, perhaps more accurately, between **Opus** and the white rhino itself. The construction of the sculpture is recorded in a series of photographs. These show that it too can be thought of as a bone structure overlaid by layers of flesh and muscle, and finally by skin. In the photographs a form which was originally angular becomes first sinuous, then completely smooth as successive layers are added.

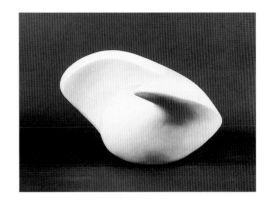

85. Shell Form maquette for marble 1982

86. 'Skeleton' of Opus 1982-3

84. Opus maquette 1982

87. Opus 1982-3

CHAPTER SIX

The white rhino drawings just described because of their connection with **Opus**, are representative of a little known aspect of Wendy Taylor's work – as private as the rest is public. These are her realistic drawings and prints, often of animals. To an ignorant eye, these might seem to be the product of a totally different artistic personality, but in fact what one finds in them are many of the same basic qualities as one finds in the sculptures – precision, refinement, tautness of line, and sometimes a feeling for the unexpected or the bizarre. As with the sculptures, things are sometimes not quite what they seem to be at first glance.

Though the drawings appear to have a certain evenness of style, more so perhaps than the sculptures, there is in fact a definite progression within the series, from the less objective to the more objective. With typical self-deprecation, Taylor claims that the drawings are not, in the strictest sense of that adjective, "accurate":

> I rarely studied the anatomy . . . or only when there was real confusion . . . In fact, there was everything wrong with my approach. I often started with the eye, as a finished detail, so that I could look at it looking at me, while I built on what I thought I saw. Or else I would detail some other part that I found fascinating, and develop the whole around it.

88. Pygmy Hamsters
1991 drawing

89. White Rhino Laying Down
1981 drawing

90. Owl 1976 drawing

91. Ibis 1976 drawing

92. Emu 1976 drawing

The coherence of style to be found in these drawings half conceals the fact that the actual media used are varied. One has to look at the sheets in some detail to detect this variety. Taylor uses charcoal, conte and pastel as well as pencil – the last, she says, is her least favourite medium, physically painful to use, and too rigid in effect, especially when covering large areas:

> I can only ever use it for small subjects (pygmy hamsters, known to me as Hampstead Ladies). Partly because my hand goes numb, which is somewhat my fault: once I start, I get obsessive, and just keep at it.

A series of drawings of birds, dating from 1976, are a summary of her earlier attitudes towards this kind of subject matter, which reminds her of people she knew. In this connection, she tells an amusing story:

> I had collected all the information I needed about one particular bird I wanted to draw, and covered a lot of distance to do so. So that evening I started work on the final drawing – and was interrupted by some chap who was driving me round the bend about some book he was trying to get me to illustrate for him – I'd foolishly done one illustration and he was determined that I was going to

93. Cayman 1983 drawing

94. Geese at Bentley 1985 drawing

do the lot. He used to call when he knew I'd be in, and I'd get livid about having to stop. My lodger let him in, and this time I was so angry that I just carried on drawing while telling him exactly where to go (I did give him a cup of coffee to take the edge off my rudeness). When he finally went, my young lodger knocked on my door to apologise for letting him in, looked at my drawing board and said: "Christ, you didn't do that when he was here, did you?" To this day even seeing a photograph of that drawing still makes me feel mad.

The point of this story is that none of the animal drawings, whether early or late, are in the least bit impersonal, though the fine finish and high degree of technical skill may perhaps deceive one into thinking the contrary:

> What I want is bulk, form, feel, even smell. I was only satisfied when I could get the drawing to "carry" all the things I wanted to say about the creature. I chose subjects because they had a mass, strength, movement, even colouring, that interested me at the time.

Keeping these comments in mind, it is not surprising to discover that her subjects have included elephants and alligators as well as rhinos. Weight and bulk, the sense that the skin has an identity of its own, are things we all associate with these creatures.

95. Pelicans 1989 drawing

Wendy Taylor has also continued to make drawings of birds, and it is interesting to compare the bird subjects done in the 1980s with those produced over a decade earlier. In the later drawings the birds often appear in pairs or groups, as if to emphasise the fact that this is a depiction primarily of a species, rather than of an individual. At the same time, there is still a strong emphasis on the absolutely particular. A pair of **Pelicans**, drawn in 1989, are shown with clipped wings. One even has a wing raised, so we can see exactly what has happened.

There are also some drawings of sheep and goats, also shown in pairs, rather than singly. The special fascination of these is their closeness (though they are different both in technique and scale) to the celebrated **Sheep** drawings made by Henry Moore towards the end of his career. The likeness brings home to one the essentially sculptural nature of Wendy Taylor's approach, despite the detailed naturalism which is also characteristic of the drawings. Both she and Moore have gone for the same quality – the hillocky appearance of the resting animal, especially when two sheep are lying close to one another, so as to create a single complex three-dimensional form.

96. Iguana – London Zoo 1986 drawing

69

Looking back from Taylor's **Sheep** drawings, made in 1988, to the portrait drawings of birds made more than a decade earlier, one realises how far her draughtsmanship has in fact progressed during the intervening period. There is no doubt that the sheep, like her elephants and rhinos, have an internal structure, a coherence of form, which is not as emphatically present in the earlier work. Taylor says she was attracted to the bird subjects by the great variety of texture to be found in their feathers and claws – they seemed a logical progression, in this respect, from the drawings of ropes which she had been making earlier.

There is one small series of drawings and prints which needs to be discussed separately, since it contains an element of pure fantasy which is absent from other depictions of animals. This series also makes direct reference to themes which are present in Taylor's sculpture. The subject is a tortoise. This was obviously likely to interest Taylor because it is concerned with the idea of a highly patterned covering or surface, with a characteristic texture, which is also to be found in the bird drawings.

97. Goats 1988 drawing

98. Sheep I 1988 drawing

99. Sheep II
(Two old ladies gossiping)
1988 drawing

70

101. Tortoise with Collapsed Brick Kite 1982 drawing

This tortoise, however, is put through a series of metamorphoses. He is seen with his shell (house) on fire as he progresses, seemingly unperturbed, across the paper – a visual pun on the cliché phrase ''getting on like a house on fire''. He is also seen, in equally unlikely fashion, flying a box kite which is attached to his shell and bobs in the air behind him. The image is all the more bizarre because the kite is made of bricks: we are in the paradoxical realm of the sculptures of the **Brick** series, where everything inverts our normal expectations. In a final image, the kite has collapsed and lies in an untidy heap of scattered bricks, while the tortoise continues his progress. The image has a bizarre quality – the kite is cut out, the string is a rigid element.

71

There is a certain surrealism about this, just as there is in the maquettes showing a box of eggs or a fruit stand made of bricks. However, the fantasy is somehow a more private one. This conforms to something which Wendy Taylor had to say about all the animal drawings, which is that they are essentially something private, done for herself. ''The trouble with public sculpture'', she says, ''is that it denies the artist a catharsis. You finish a piece, and perhaps there's a dedication ceremony, then suddenly it's not yours anymore – in a certain sense you've nothing to show for all those months of effort, nothing that remains with you, not even a catalogue of the kind a dealer might produce for an exhibition. At some dedication ceremonies I've been to, you get the feeling that the artist who made the piece, who *imagined* it, is already an irrelevance. People are thinking of the person it commemorates, or the directors of the firm responsible for commissioning it, or the speech about to be made by His Worship the Mayor. The sculpture itself has somehow arrived out of thin air. Making the drawings of animals, and keeping them, is a kind of compensation.''

The work in which this sense of privacy is most forcibly expressed, however, is not a drawing, but a set of etchings, the exquisite **Little Black Box of Mushrooms** (1981). Wendy Taylor's interest in printmaking goes back a long way:

> I started etching at evening classes at St Martin's. In those days, activities of that sort were very much frowned upon by the sculpture department, and in any case you couldn't just go and work in other departments as you can now. I wanted to do some more prints – and to learn about etching – so a friend and I signed on for classes without telling anyone, just as though we were ''outside evening students'' one evening a week!

102. Little Black Box of Mushrooms
1981 etching

Later, when I was teaching printmaking at one of the colleges, I had access to an etching-press again. I worked in tea-breaks, lunch hours and evenings. I started with some images taken from sketches I had made of a friend's topiary garden. I then found I didn't like the fixed edge, so decided to take the plates to the studio and cut them up. After that the edge became the actual edge of the image – for me it had a marvellous tactile quality. What I loved was the "black" of etching, and shaping the plate meant that I could get the strength of black I wanted without spending ages cleaning up the part of the plate area which I wanted to be white. The mushroom series developed out of this.

In fact the mushroom etchings can also be thought of as sculptures, or at least reliefs, in miniature. Each form literally bites into the white of the paper. What these images record is something very personal:

> I've always had a fascination with mushrooms, fungi of all sorts (memories of childhood – staying with my grandmother in the country, and cycling off at dawn in the mist to the meadows by the river to hunt for mushrooms). I like the variations of texture and form. I used to make a lot of drawings showing details of walls with fungi and ferns growing on them. I did this again and again as a child. It was an amazing world in a few square inches.

The final gesture, after making the mushroom etchings, was to find a way of quite literally closing them off from plain view. This is the additional purpose of the box made to enclose the set – it protects, and it also conceals. It is impossible to think of anything much further from public art.

103. Culham Bird 1983 etching

104. Tree Walk 1981 etching

CHAPTER SEVEN

The years 1984 and 1985 demonstrate the wide range of different commissions Taylor was now being asked to undertake. There is a marked contrast, for instance, between **Network** (1984-5), and **Geo I** and **Geo II** (both 1984-6), though the notion of the ''global'' is inherent in all three. **Network** is entirely abstract. It is also three-dimensional, whereas **Geo I** and **Geo II** are figurative reliefs.

Making **Network** is not one of the sculptural enterprises that Taylor remembers with the greatest fondness, even though the finished result was impressive and satisfied the client. The sculpture was a commission for STC plc, for their new headquarters building in New Southgate, North London, and was subsequently dedicated by them to the memory of their Managing Director, John Smith, who had died while he was abroad on the service of the company.

The sculpture consists of a three-dimensional grid of aluminium tubes, which together make up a sphere which is ten feet in diameter. At the end of each tube there is a hologram – there are 720 of these in all, each depicting a four-core optical cable. When the piece is illuminated with white light the holograms shine with the colours of the spectrum, and the hues change with each shift of viewing angle. The basic structure of the hologram is thus very much in the Constructivist tradition, while the details pay tribute to STC's involvement with high technology.

Describing her approach to the commission, Taylor says:

> Starting with the original conception (which was to incorporate references to communication and the worldwide nature of STC's activities), I did some research at the Science Museum which indicated various approaches to the theme. I chose not to involve movement because of the problem of noise, however minimal; the use of lights and electricity would create unnecessary maintenance problems, although a changing image incorporated into the sculpture seemed important. To create an image expressing global communication led to an interconnecting network theme with a sphere indicative of the world.

The difficulties Taylor experienced in making and installing the piece were considerable. As she points out, they are typical of some of the pitfalls which lie in wait for the creator of public sculpture.

105. Network maquette 1983

106. Network installation 1984

A public sculpture is almost invariably a one-off. It may involve processes new to the sculptor and almost always entails making use of outside contractors for some of the manufacturing processes. In this case two of the companies involved went into liquidation during the fabrication of the work – one was the aluminium casting company making the solid junctions for the tubes; the other was the factory she initially chose as a place where she could carry out the actual fabrication.

Other difficulties arose when it was time for the finished sculpture (which weighs one and a quarter tons) to be installed. The building was what is called in the construction business a "design and build" project. That is, the architect and builder were employed as a single unit, rather than working as separate entities. Because of this, the architect was able to make changes at will during the building process, so long as they did not affect the overall budget. Such changes, however, inevitably affected Taylor's own limited fixed budget.

108. Geo I 1985-6

109. Geo II 1985-6

76

Her position was made the more difficult by the fact that she had been brought into the project through an agent and was technically a subcontractor.

One result of the division of responsibilities was that the actual suspension system for the sculpture was designed by the architect's own in-house engineers. Taylor had grave doubts about this, but her protests were ignored. When the sculpture was put in place, it started to spin (as she had feared) and the suspension cable began to unwind. Because of the threat to safety, Taylor had to have a closing order put on the building until the error had been corrected.

Geo I and **Geo II** were much less complex from a technical point of view. The commission came to Wendy Taylor after she won a limited competition. The client was the National Farmers' Union, and the location was another new headquarters building. Taylor says that the reliefs were rooted in a job she had rather reluctantly undertaken a year previously, which was to design a bronze medal for the Swedish company E.S.A.B., whose founder had been the inventor of arc (electric) welding. "Actually", she remembers, "I found it fascinating, exploring the enormity of two inches in diameter".

The site the NFU building offered was very impressive – on a staircase, with good natural light. It was, she thought, an opportunity to explore further the possibilities offered by relief sculpture, which she had glimpsed when working on the medal a year earlier.

110. Artist setting out templates for Geo II 1985

Looking at the physical situation, she decided it was not merely a relief which was appropriate, but the circle form taken from the medal. This had two advantages – one practical, one symbolic. The shape, self-sufficient and contained, dealt with the problem created by pillars which interrupted the view when one was walking up and down the staircase. It was also an image of containment – appropriate since one of the NFU's most important functions was to act as an insurer, offering farmers protection against the ravages wrought by the elements: wind, rain and lightning.

The roundels – made of polished and satin finished aluminium to match the stainless steel railings and other details of the staircase – are partly cut out, so that the wall behind remains visible, and partly in layered, very shallow relief. Taylor decided that anything which projected too far from the wall might seem threatening,

111. Existing subway unit, Basildon, Essex

112. Roundacre Scheme Phase I, 1:100 scale model showing underpasses, paving layout, central feature, seating, etc. 1985-8

and make the experience of walking up and down the staircase uncomfortable. At the same time, however, she wanted to choose forms which took full advantage of the great flood of natural light descending from above. One of the roundels features a lightning flash; the other rain driving down diagonally from the clouds, with rippling waves beneath to symbolise the power of the wind.

The two commissions I have just mentioned fall within a range of expectation – they are what we expect of public sculpture in the sense that they are objects designed to have a relationship with and animate a particular space (which may, of course, be either indoor or outdoor). Wendy Taylor's later work for Basildon goes a long way beyond this range. It involves aspects of planning, architecture and landscaping, and also something resembling mural painting, in addition to sculpture. If the scheme possessed strong political content (as it might have done in Mexico, for example, where Diego Rivera undertook some projects which are not wholly dissimilar), her work for Basildon would be more famous than it is at the moment.

The commission there (1985-91) arose from the success of **Compass Bowl** (1980), which has already been described, and also perhaps from Taylor's typically forthright criticisms of the underpasses which led to this. The Basildon Development Corporation now wanted to improve the capacity and efficiency of a major roundabout constructed in 1958, which was now becoming overloaded at peak times. They decided to replace it with two roundabouts, connected by a short stretch of dual carriageway. The southern roundabout – the first phase – involved the construction of three large subways, central low level footpaths, and also cycletracks, which between them would provide complete segregation of motor traffic from pedestrians and cyclists. The second phase contained a long subway with a footpath and cycletrack leading to a new road bridge. Pedestrians and cyclists passed under this on their way to a park called Gloucester Park. The official design brief given to Taylor read as follows:

> To analyse the Development Corporation's requirements and from the Chief Engineer's outline proposals to develop a scheme design to illustrate the size and character of the entire project both individually and in relationship to surrounding areas. This design is to include proposals for the shape and finished form of the structures, paved areas and landscaped areas, together with choice of materials, colour and texture of all finished surfaces. To consult fully with the Chief Engineer's Department and to attend design group meetings to ensure feasibility and economic viability of design.

Later, Wendy Taylor's responsibilities were extended to cover the construction stages, in order to ensure that

113. Installation of underpass sections (Phase I) 1988

114. Detail of underpass showing external finishes (Phase II) 1989-90

her design concepts were properly carried out. She was specifically given responsibility for on-site inspection.

What she proposed was that the two phases of the scheme should be treated rather differently. The first phase was close to the Civic Centre and the Railway Station, and she recommended that it be treated in a fairly formal manner:

> I wanted the space to be an enclave in its own right with a distinctive character, not just a means of crossing main roads. I wanted to create a pleasant place where people could meet and sit. Because of its important relationship to the main civic area I chose a grey and silver scheme throughout, providing a contrast to the second phase, which by virtue of its environs required, I felt, a more informal approach.

One of the most radical decisions involved in the commission was to allow Taylor to design an entirely new shape of underpass, semi-elliptical in section, rather than the conventional box.

> The shape not only looked more inviting but actually gave pedestrians more elbow room; it admitted more daylight, increased the efficiency of the interior lighting, and permitted application of a continuous decorative finish to walls and roof. User safety would be increased by the elimination of vertical walls, against which it is easier for an attacker to push his victim.

> Continuous strip lighting along the crown of the ellipse, and stainless steel trim to the portals – a material used for its further link with the overall scheme – were adopted with the additional advantage of overcoming problems often encountered with conventional designs, such as graffiti.

In the subways, differing shades of grey were used to delineate footpaths and cycletracks.

Wendy Taylor designed an armillary sundial as a centrepiece for the landscaped area contained within the elevated roundabout. This, like the compass in **Compass Bowl**, was intended to give the area its own identity.

> The sundial [Taylor notes] is man's oldest astronomical instrument, yet its functions can be incorporated within clean modern forms. The shapes here are "modern" but they don't rouse the same adversarial reaction that a functionless piece of sculpture might from certain members of the general public.

The second phase of the scheme was treated differently, with much less sense of formality. The subway leading to it has the same elliptical section as is used elsewhere, but the tiling pattern features a tree motif. The trees meet overhead, so that the subway becomes a kind of avenue. The underpass under the new bridge – the route which leads to Gloucester Park – is decorated with a different motif, more emphatically

115. Underpass entrance (Phase I) 1988

used. The route under the bridge is bordered by a
revetment. At one entrance, this has a mosaic of
cobbles set in concrete, while under the bridge the
revetment is white concrete with inlaid black
silhouettes, also in concrete. In both cases the subjects
are the same – boldly drawn full-size likenesses of
animals – a rhino, an ostrich, an elephant, a baboon, a
camel – all running towards the park. In some cases the
subjects are the same as those which Wendy Taylor had
already used for the ''private'' drawings made on her
visits to the zoo. One can see how these studies,
without preplanning on her part, fed directly into the
work she did at Basildon, just as one can see that the
early **Gazebo** is in some respects the ancestor of the
underpasses she designed as part of the same
commission.

What the work of this period in Taylor's career does is
raise a number of fascinating questions about the links
between public art on the one hand, and purely personal
art on the other. Late twentieth-century attitudes to this
are extremely contradictory. On the one hand
Modernism has reinforced an attitude already prevalent
amongst the Romantics of the nineteenth century,

116. Roundacre Scheme Phase I, Basildon, Essex 1989

which is that the artist must work only for himself or herself – that every artwork must be a purely individual expression. Carried to an extreme, this means that valid public art is no longer possible.

This is, however, contradicted by the fact that the artist's supposedly private products more and more tend to be purchased for public display – the true home of the avant-garde artwork is a museum, not a private collection.

It is also contradicted by the fact that many twentieth-century artists are determined to make what they do into public statements – their art may, for example, be about politics, or ecology, or feminist issues.

The works by Taylor discussed in this chapter do none of these things. There is, nevertheless, a real sense, especially in the work done for Basildon, that this is art which is not just "public" in the narrow sense that it is out in public, and in this case commissioned by a public body, but something actually done *for* the public. In intention it is meliorative – designed, in a very specific way, to improve the quality of people's lives. It differs from the public statements referred to above because it does not simply comment (and it must be recognised that such comments are usually negative – protests or complaints about what is happening), it actually goes out and does something. By doing so, it to some extent calls into question the Modernist ethos.

117. Installation of animal fresco concrete panels (Phase II) 1989

118. Section showing tree pattern tiling in underpass (Phase II) 1990

sections. In each case, one side of the tube is cut at a right angle, the other on a diagonal. Perhaps the most typical feature of the sculpture is the fact that these tubular sections appear to lift away from the granite base which supports them. This gives the sculpture strong rhythmic impetus. While there is no overt illusionism, as there is with the sculptures of the **Chain** and **Brick** series, the spectator gets the feeling that the sculpture is in motion. The two sections seem to have linked arms and to be engaged in a sort of whirling dance.

The next piece, **Landscape** (1986), was a response to an entirely different set of physical circumstances, though it too was the product of a limited competition. What was wanted on this occasion was a large wall relief:

> The building [Taylor recalls] was very good in design, with a superb roof line and excellent interior detailing. The inside, as I picked up from the drawings (the building itself was still under construction) was to be very complicated with "loud" finishes. The architect had a very fixed view about what should be there – he wanted a long abstract relief panel. Another problem was that the wall was extremely long, which made the space itself rather tunnel like.

Trying to find solutions for some of these purely practical problems, she began to think about what the client – ICI – actually did, and how the building was going to be used. It was in fact to be a conference headquarters for the company's Plant Protection Division, which deals with worldwide crop research and development. This seemed to her the perfect opportunity to develop further some of the ideas she had already used in **Geo I** and **Geo II**, and also (more specifically) in some sketches she had already made for an etching she wanted to do. The subject was a vast field she used to visit each year, with the lines made by the plough seemingly reaching to the horizon. In these circumstances the architect's prejudice in favour of something entirely abstract ought (she felt) to be put aside.

> I developed my existing Oxfordshire field and tree line to incorporate a more visual skyline. I felt it was essential that the wall be seen through the work so as to try to break up the long, narrow effect of the area. The wall surface had a curious suede texture which worked well with the smooth aluminium surfaces chosen for the relief, and the aluminium also went well with the silver suspended ceiling.

123. Pharos 1986

124. Nexus 1986

125. Landscape 1986

126. Tree of the Wood 1986

127. Ceres 1986-7

The finished result was so much liked that Wendy Taylor was asked to do further work in the same building. **Tree of the Wood** (1986) is a witty solution to an even more intractable problem than that presented by the site for **Landscape**.

> My first reaction on seeing the area was to turn it down. Although it cried out for something, I just couldn't think what. It was the wall beside a staircase; the surface treatment was white, and the thickest texture I had ever seen. Partly because of this depth of texture the banister rail was very large and placed at quite a distance from the wall, to protect you from being shredded if you fell down the stairs. The colour of the wood and carpet, let alone the intense white of the walls, made it difficult to imagine where an image might fit in.

To try and solve the problem, she built a working model of the staircase in order to be able to study all the possible viewpoints. She already knew that she wanted to use the same colour wood as the existing banisters, but still nothing seemed to work. "It was only when I got a sample of the wood to stare at and started to wonder how many American ash trees had been needed for the job of making those massive banisters that it all started to fall into place." Her solution was logical and utterly unexpected – to turn the banisters themselves into the image of a gigantic tree:

> The challenge, as I saw it, was to make an artwork which could stand in its own right, but which would also be unique to that space. It would have been a darned sight easier to do other things than to have to persuade ICI to have their brand new, extraordinarily expensive, beautifully made banisters sawn up – but they were very brave.

Wendy Taylor's third and final commission for the same building was **Ceres** (1986-7), a relief representing a plant and its roots in aluminium, made for the top floor, board-room level staircase. (Ceres is, of course, the name of the Roman goddess of agriculture.) She also made maquettes for stained-glass windows for the boardroom itself, picking up and varying the theme of **Landscape**, but these, unfortunately, were never carried out.

1986 also saw the beginning of another monumental sundial, the **Globe Sundial**, which won a competition organised by Swansea City Council for a sculpture for the new Swansea Maritime Quarter which was a reclamation of the old and now disused dock area of the city. On this occasion Wendy Taylor imagined her sundial as a globe, a replica of the earth itself, with its axis parallel to the earth's own axis. One tells the time by means of the fins on the globe – the hour is indicated by the one which casts, not the longest, but the shortest shadow. These fins give a rather sea-urchin-like appearance to the sculpture as a whole –

something not inappropriate in the circumstances, as the sculpture stands immediately beside the sea wall, with the beach beyond.

Taylor's major work of 1987 was the monumental steel sculpture **Spirit of Enterprise**, sited in London's Docklands. The form is an ingenious geographical metaphor. The looped shape derives from the contour of the river Thames itself, as it encircles the Isle of Dogs. Taylor has used this idea as the basis for a piece which has quite a close formal relationship with some of the sculptures in the **Brick** series, and also with **Pharos** and **Phoenix**. Like **Timepiece** higher up the river, **Spirit of Enterprise** has become one of the emblems of the ''new'' London, built on reclaimed dockyard sites.

The sculpture in fact began life as the **Docklands Business Enterprise Award** (1985), a trophy in maquette form. It had, however, always been understood when the trophy was commissioned that the sculpture would be made full-scale once a suitable site was found. The arguments which followed, concerning the siting of the work, reflect, in paradigmatic form, some of the difficulties which bedevil prestigious commissions for public sculpture. There was a conflict of interests and also a conflict of points of view.

The original site was to have been on dry land, but with a reflecting pool, like that provided for **Octo**. This was abandoned because it was thought that the place chosen, and therefore the sculpture, might be vulnerable to development as land values in the Docklands rose. It was then decided to place the piece out in the dock. Here a conflict arose between

128. Stained Glass Window 1:20 scale model 1987

129. **Detail of Globe Sundial 1987**

130. **Globe Sundial 1987**

aesthetics and politics. The London Docklands Development Corporation, which was responsible for the commission, naturally did not want to see the sculpture appropriated (kidnapped might be a better term) by any one firm in particular, simply because it was in close proximity to their premises. Wendy Taylor, on the other hand, was understandably anxious that the work should have an immediately comprehensible relationship to its surroundings, and most of all to the buildings near to it. An impassioned series of arguments followed:

> My argument was that it was immaterial at the end of the day what building the sculpture was next to. The important thing was that it should look right in scale – a large plaque on the quayside would surely be the solution.

> Many site visits ensued, the position crept nearer to the ideal spot. I suggested that it be decided by the throw of a stone (much practiced in private, I hasten to add). This was agreed; X marked the spot on the plan – I drove home elated.

> I went to see the foundation pile when it was being installed and to my horror it was being put in the wrong place. I was wild. I found out that the X had been moved (albeit not a lot, but...) without my being informed. I have to drive past the work on a regular basis and it still irks me every time! Perhaps I sound very petty about the siting saga, but to me it is so critical. I always feel the misjudgement reflects on me, though I *can* understand about the "ownership" aspect.

133. Spirit of Enterprise
(Docklands Enterprise) 1987

131. Spirit of Enterprise maquette 1987

132. Two drawings showing original proposed site 1985

92

CHAPTER NINE

The **Whirlies** (1988), Wendy Taylor's second sculpture
for the East Kilbride Development Corporation at Peel
Park is, as she herself says, the most difficult of all her
works to describe, or to illustrate satisfactorily.

> The brief [Taylor says] was that there was no genuine
> sense of arrival at the main entrance. There were simply
> lots of fast roads, of the motorway type, converging at a
> huge roundabout. Even the standard motorway sign up
> there was frequently being stolen for scrap, so people had
> no exact idea of where they were, or what they were
> coming to.

The piece, therefore, has no specific message – it is
neither an allegory nor a commemoration. Its job is to
provide a sense of place, and at the same time Taylor
wanted it to activate certain kinetic sensations – those
of speed, direction, coming to somewhere, going round.
The sculpture could have no front or back – every
viewpoint was equally important. And it had to occupy –
colonise might be a better verb – an enormous space.
The roundabout where it is sited measures 262 feet by
205 feet.

Wendy Taylor's solution to the problem was to create
five stainless steel spheres, each eight feet in diameter
and of honeycomb construction. The spheres are
mirror-finished and set at different angles so as to catch
the light; they appear to roll around as the spectator
approaches. Where earlier monumental sculptures –
those made for city piazzas during the Italian
Renaissance, for example – had the pedestrian almost
exclusively in mind, the **Whirlies** are primarily designed
to be seen from vehicular traffic, and derive kinetic
energy from the speed of the vehicle itself.

Careful lighting tests were necessary to make sure that
the sculpture had the effect intended, and Taylor
remembers these with some vividness:

> The Scots are amazing. During the final lighting tests *in
> situ*, we humped a generator round with all the electrical
> gear in the middle of the night in torrential rain. Each
> movement had to be checked, then viewed from mid- and
> long-distances. It took hours – but in spite of Wellington
> boots (for those of us who had them) filling up with water,
> and despite the fact that everyone was wet right through
> to their underwear, we carried on until the job was
> finished. There was no shirking: it was all regarded as an
> adventure. Something quite different from the tea-break
> and stop-for-weather rules which prevail on the other side
> of the border.

135. Maquette of one of the five spheres making up The Whirlies 1988

136. The Whirlies 1988

137. Phoenix 1989-90

138. Balloons montage 1973

Two more works for the same patron followed, **Pharos II** and **Phoenix** (1988-90). The commissions arose directly from the success of the original **Pharos**, which had become part of the identity of Peel Park, appearing on signs and even on lapel badges. This very success created certain practical problems. The new campus now had a very visible front entrance, but also, at the rear of the site, a back door which remained anonymous and difficult to find. Wendy Taylor produced **Phoenix**, which was an alternative version of **Pharos**, but based on a star form. In the end, however, she was to make a second version of **Pharos** for Peel Park, but the East Kilbride Development Corporation commissioned the new sculpture for an alternative site. Taylor says she is particularly pleased, in the case of **Phoenix**, with the way in which the sculpture is lit – the product of much experiment. The lights are powerful beams which are broken up by the shapes of the sculpture to create beautiful patterns in the sky.

Pilot Kites (1988) was the product of a competition for a sculpture for the new airport buildings at Norwich. Taylor gave much thought to the actual siting, basing her ideas on her own frequent experience of airports. Indoor areas, she noted, already tended to be cluttered and restless – a sculpture would add to the crowding. A prime outdoor site which had been suggested would, she felt, be better used for advertising which would bring in revenue. She settled for a position at the entrance to one of the car parks. She wanted the sculpture to be raised well off the ground, so that it would serve as a landmark. Her solution, having chosen the site, was to make a version of the original box kites used at primitive airports to indicate wind direction. For her, the motif also had something quite personal about it. She had had a passion for kites ever since she was a child. In fact, she still owns a number and flies them when she can.

In a sculptural sense, **Pilot Kites** has something in common with the **Chain** pieces, since objects which are in fact heavy (the kites naturally had to be made of metal) are supported by the elements which seem to tether them and stop them from flying away. An even closer parallel than the one with the chain sculptures is supplied by a maquette for an unexecuted sculpture (1978) which was to have been sited on the South Bank in London. Here Taylor envisaged three silvery balloons made of metal, apparently tethered, though in actual fact held up, by rope with a metal core. The maquette offers an example of the consistent way in which her sculpture has developed, and shows the way in which she has been able to make public projects into personal means of expression.

139. Pilot Kites (one of two) 1987

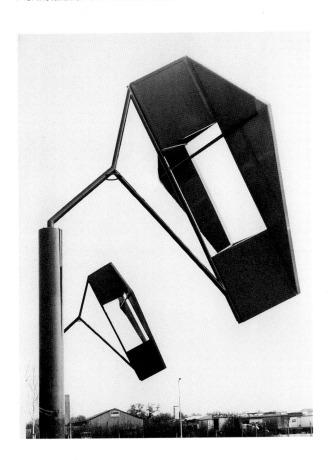

140. Installation of Pilot Kites 1988

The kite forms at Norwich, by their very nature, were bound to take the full brunt of wind stresses. Taylor originally planned to make the work in aluminium, and had anxious consultations with her engineers. They did their calculations and told her that winds up to fifty miles per hour should present no problem. Stronger winds, meteorological records showed, occurred only every fifty years or so. For the sculptor, this was not good enough. At her own expense she changed the specification to stainless steel, manufactured to aircraft standards. A heavy gale followed the day after she made the decision. This was followed by a second gale, soon after the sculptures were put up. Equipment at the airport registered gusts of up to 100 miles per hour.

> When the hurricane occurred, I spent a sleepless night wondering which works might have problems – the **Pilot Kites** were uppermost in my mind. In the end I couldn't stand the suspense. I telephoned Norwich the next day. I was told that my kites had put on quite a show – spinning etc. – but that, in spite of much local structural damage close by, they had come through intact, quite unscathed. I think a lot of the credit was due to all those engineering calculations made by others.

Pilot Kites, in turn, has an affinity with another, much smaller sculpture of the same epoch, **Silver Fountain** (1988). Taylor engagingly describes this as ''a crazy idea'', but in reality the sculpture is an ingenious solution to an intractable problem. Its link with **Pilot Kites** is that it is another, though very different, example of frozen motion.

The sculpture came about in the following way. The architects of the new British Oxygen Company Cryoplant offices in Guildford, who already knew Taylor's work, approached her to provide something for a small seating area, circular and open to the sky. A water feature had originally been planned for the space, but it became clear that this could cause problems. The site itself seemed to call for height, and the area was quite windy. A tall fountain jet would inevitably drench anyone sitting near it or passing close to it.

The solution was to have a fountain but to make it of polished steel: the appearance of water flowing, without the inconveniences attendant on the reality. The sculpture also seemed to incorporate a nice allusion to what the Cryoplant Division did: its business was the containment of liquid gasses. Of course in the British climate even a steel fountain would not be completely static – or not in an outdoor location. When it rained, the drops would animate it; if there was a real cold snap, with freezing temperatures, then the piece would drip with icicles.

141. Silver Fountain 1988   142. Fireflow 1988

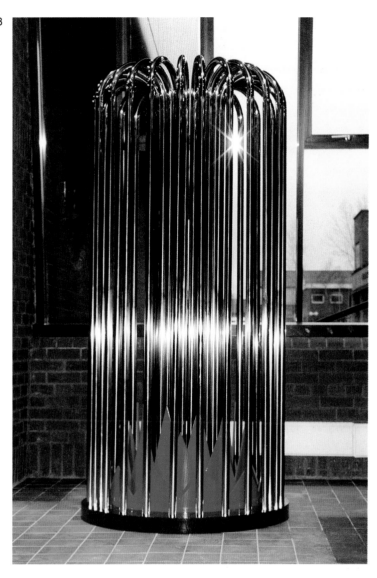

143. Jester maquette 1988

Silver Fountain led to **Fireflow** (1988), a different and larger version of the same idea made for the public area of the new headquarters building of the Strathclyde Fire Brigade. Here the conceit of frozen motion is pushed even further, with "flames" rising from the bottom of the piece, to be symbolically contained by jets of "water" streaming from its top. Taylor was especially touched and pleased by the reception given to this piece by the firemen, who had begun with strong reservations about the whole idea of "modern art". In the end they were so pleased with the result that they formally presented her with the Strathclyde Fire Brigade shield.

Illusions – the gap between what we see and what we think we see – are familiar currency in Taylor's art. There is also, however, her persistent interest in three-dimensional form – the way in which it changes (though not illusionistically) when the same form is seen from different aspects. This is the message of **Octo**, for example, which is clearly a key piece in Taylor's personal development.

144. Artist working on full-scale Jester 1992

The true successor of **Octo** is **Jester** (maquette 1988, full-scale mock-up 1991-2). This is perhaps the supreme example, so far at least, of Taylor's skill in using twisting, ribbon-like shapes to create abstract forms which change dramatically with even the slightest shift in the angle of view. It still awaits a commission, and a site for the full-scale version, not least because Taylor herself has strong views about how the work should be viewed. She feels that it needs to be visible from above, as well as from all sides.

Jester has an obvious relationship with **Continuum** (1989-90) which also makes use of a twisting strip as its basic motif, though in this case the strip is much thicker and meets the base at two points rather than just one. Despite this link, **Continuum** is unusual in Taylor's work in several respects. Chief among these are the material (marble), and the fact that it was made as a private rather than a public commission. Like **The Travellers**, it is sited in private grounds. The piece, like most contemporary sculpture in marble (including the late work of Henry Moore) was made by professional carvers in the marble workshops at Pietrasanta in Italy. However, it was later altered and refined by the sculptor. Taylor, whose maternal grandfather was a stonemason, has great admiration for the professional stonecarvers (for many it is a family trade, handed down for generations from father to son), but she instances

145. Artist working on Continuum maquette 1989

obtaining exactly the result desired when using artisan help of this sort, however skilled. She wonders aloud about the freedom of interpretation a number of celebrated contemporary sculptors seem to have allowed their helpers in similar circumstances. She agrees with the stonemasons themselves that what is needed is firstly an accurate maquette, and secondly close communication with those carrying out the job.

Continuum, which is the epitome of sophisticated smoothness, thanks to its continuously flowing lines and seductive, slightly translucent material, makes a telling contrast with a sculpture very close to it in date, **Oxide** (1989-90). This illustrates another aspect of Taylor's talent – her responsiveness to new materials as well as to widely different sets of circumstances. **Oxide** is comparatively small (it may be built on a larger scale at a later date). Made of concrete, it was designed as a trophy for the Bayer "Colour in Architecture" award. Appropriately, the piece itself shows a rich use of colour:

> Bayer kindly gave me dozens of small jars containing raw pigment, many beautiful rich earthy colours. From the range, I decided to choose those which worked together and make them the basis for a *very* three-dimensional object – something which had no obvious top, bottom or sides, which would express the idea of "evenness" in the way the actual weight was distributed.

Taylor notes that the image is deeply rooted in her early work, specifically in drawings done in the 1960s in which she made use of overlapping images. She also notes that the element of illusionism is present, but partly concealed, in the sense that sculpture both contradicts one's visual expectations (through the operation of colour), and also one's expectations about the actual material of which it is made:

> I enjoy these challenges [she remarks] because I see my work as being like a tree. It has lots of ideas or branches, and no branch is ever quite finished with; there is always something more to be explored. Either an opportunity presents itself, or one is seized by some immediate interest, and these give one the chance to explore further.

147. Oxide 1989-90

During the 1990s, Wendy Taylor's work has continued to develop along lines already laid down in the 1970s and 1980s. One striking thing about recent enterprises is their consistency – but consistency is always combined with a readiness to accept new challenges. Some of her commissions also exemplify the many difficulties which still lie in wait for the public sculptor. In particular, they show the amount of time which has to pass before a particular job reaches fruition.

Taylor's environmental work in Basildon, for example, led in 1989 to a commission for similar work at Barking. There are two projects. One concerns walkways and underpasses being built in connection with the Barking Northern Relief Road. The underpasses form part of a main school route, used by a local community which is predominantly Asian. What was needed, Taylor felt, was something to give life and character to an area which seemed at first sight extremely drab. She noticed, however, that the surrounding area was full of self-seeded sweet peas which, in turn, attracted great numbers of the common blue butterfly: ''The markings are wonderful – the male and female are quite different and individuals all vary within the species.''

She therefore designed a series of boldly conceived glass mosaics featuring these butterflies, plus a further series of tiled mosaics showing trees, not unlike those she had made for Basildon. The mosaics are now complete, but are still awaiting installation.

Another scheme, for a different site in Barking, involves reshaping the whole pedestrian approach to the new Goresbrook Sports Centre. At the time of writing this is awaiting approval from the Department of the Environment.

Rope Circle (1990) and **Anchorage** (1991) are essentially two halves of the same story. **Rope Circle** was commissioned for the redevelopment of Salford Docks, Manchester. The form was suggested by three things: the dockside setting, the numerous drawings and maquettes of ropes which Wendy Taylor had been making since the 1970s, in step with her studies of chains and other dockland impedimenta, and most of all by the proposed site. One purpose was to draw people's attention to the view. The sculpture served as a punctuation mark in the urban landscape, but was also something for the spectator to walk round, and walk beyond. It could be looked through as well as looked at.

Rough setting out of butterflies for mosaic colour coding

148. Proposal for pedestrian route, Northern Relief Road, Barking, Essex 1:20 scale model 1989

earlier. Taylor describes it as one of her happier experiences in terms of personal relationships, and also as one of her most difficult works to make, from a purely technical viewpoint:

> On reflection, I could never have made the work before. Everything was pushed to extreme limits: me, the materials, the engineering, the other people involved. It needed every scrap of all my years of experience not to give up in despair.

In some ways, the making process became a kind of parable of Britain's industrial decline:

> As the sculpture got bigger and sections were added, I moved factories to accommodate the process. The last place I was in was in the very process of folding up. I watched the men going, the machinery being sold for scrap. One man was still polishing and oiling his lathe as it was being lifted onto the back of a lorry; he had worked on it all his life.

> I worked there every day, and they gave me an old locker and made me tea. **Square Piece** was a bizarre presence in the surroundings. When it was nearing completion a lot of people from the whole trading estate came, with cameras of every shape and size. I was given two giant pairs of callipers by the men before they left, because they thought I would find them useful, and as something to remember them by . . . Things that happened still move me to tears.

Square Piece, created in these surroundings, was destined for the United States. It was commissioned for the grounds of a house designed by an internationally famous architect: a building which is one of the icons of International Modernist architecture:

> Although I had seen many photographs of the building, I had no idea until I got there on the initial site visit of the proportions, the attention to detail, the perfect lines. I was alone there and just revelled in the sheer visual pleasure of it all.

She was given complete freedom over the siting of the piece, even the right to move or plant trees if she thought this was necessary. She decided that what she wanted to do was to "frame" some of the views (as **Rope Circle** would have done on the site originally chosen), and at the same time to make something which would work as an entity in its own right. To get the proportions right, she built a timber mock-up to the exact size while she was there, and looked at it from every important viewpoint: "How you would see it when you first arrived, how it would be when you were close, in fact from every angle." When she accepted the commission, she decided that everything had to be made in England, even the York stone paving detail, leaving only the foundations to be installed on site. She was determined that the work would be as finely engineered as the house itself and this needed

154. Fabrication of Sheffield Sundial 1991

155. Sundial maquette 1991

156. Sheffield Sundial 1991

111

157. Preparation of Square Piece prior to being moved for crating

hands-on involvement throughout. **Square Piece** now occupies its place exactly as she originally imagined it:

> Beyond **Square Piece** is a river. The river regularly rises in flood, so there will be many occasions when it will seem to rise out of the water or ice like King Arthur's sword, Excalibur, rising out of the lake. Or it will be seen amid the stark whiteness of the snow, with which the area is completely covered during the long winter. The patron was really pleased, and I hope loves the piece as much as I do.

It seems fitting that **Square Piece** stands last in this book, for more than one reason. It not only demonstrates, very clearly, the element of continuity in Taylor's career, and the extraordinary coherence of her aesthetic, but it also stands as a kind of personal monument.

What it commemorates, in purely personal terms, are the difficulties she has had to overcome. It is immensely difficult to make a career as a public sculptor in a modern industrial democracy. All the relationships are more complicated than they were in the Renaissance (when, heaven knows, as both records and anecdotes show, they were often complicated enough). Among the obstacles are finance, lack of information about contemporary art and what it does, and lack of agreed aesthetic standards amongst the "professionals" – by which I mean artists, teachers, art historians and critics. Taylor has had to struggle against the additional obstacle of being a woman. We are still not accustomed to the idea of women artists claiming an equal place with their male colleagues, though it has at least become customary to pay lip service to the idea.

The mark of Wendy Taylor's success is the large number of works she has succeeded in getting made. It is also their quality, and the way in which each of them both responds to, and at the same time subtly alters, the nature of the site which it occupies. Furthermore, these sculptures, unlike so much contemporary art, are built to last. Wendy Taylor has no patience with imperfect workmanship, and ill-concealed disdain for people who think that careless workmanship is a necessary mark of artistic genius. Her sculptures as well as being works of art, are always fine examples of industrial craft – this, I think, is one of the reasons why the public responds to them. Like Taylor herself, they think that if a thing is worth doing at all it is worth doing well. Certainly she has had extraordinary success in making sculpture which has found its place in the public psyche. People may not know who made a particular work, but that work has, nevertheless, often become the symbol of the place where it stands.

158. Square Piece 1990-1

SCULPTURE and Maquettes

The catalogue of works does not include many pieces which have been lost or where no proper record exists.

1964

MACMANHINE 1964

Several untitled pieces involving soft and hard forms

SEA 1964

SECOND THOUGHT ON SUMMER 1964

No Bird Soars Too High if He Soars with his Own Wings
Maquette for proposed sculpture at Blackbird Leys School

1965

NUCLEUS 1965

MOBILE 1965

LATE EAST SUMMER 1965

PLANE CONFORMITY 1965

CAPTIVE SPHEROIDS 1965

ENCLOSED STIGMA 1965

SPRING 1965

THE SONG OF SOLOMON II 1965

GERMINATION 1965

ENCLOSED STIGMA

GERMINATION

PLANE CONFORMITY

SPRING

1966

THE SERIES 1965-6
I Yellow/Green (originally Red)
99cm x 111.7cm x 15cm (39″ x 44″ x 6″)

II Blue/Green
147.3cm x 91.4cm x 40.6cm (58″ x 36″ x 16″)

III Purple/Green
251.4cm x 106.6cm x 12.7cm (99″ x 42″ x 5″)

IV Orange/Yellow/Red
248.9cm x 152.4cm x 12.7cm (98″ x 60″ x 5″)

V Light Green/Dark Green
43.1cm x 212.5cm x 91.4cm x 10.1cm (17″ x 84″ x 36″ x 4″)

VI Turquoise/Green
213.5cm x 111.7cm x 12.7cm (84″ x 44″ x 5″)

BLUE SPILL 1965-6
H 457.2cm (15′)

SKY DUNES 1966
L 121.9cm (48″)

DAYBREAK 1966
H 198.2cm x W 20.3cm x L 121.9cm (78″ x 8″ x 48″)

DEEP GLOW 1966
H 182.9cm x W 20.3cm x L 203.2cm (72″ x 8″ x 80″)

Purple/Green

Orange/Yellow/Red

SKY DUNES

Light Green/Dark Green

1 9 6 7

CALENDULA 1966-7
Each unit 76.2cm diameter (30″)

CALTHAE 1967
Each section 168cm diameter (66″)

Untitled Maquette

Untitled Maquette

CALENDULA

1 9 6 8

Nocturne Maquette

NOCTURNE 1968
213.4cm x 213.4cm x 45.8cm (7′ x 7′ x 18″)

CHEVRON 1968
Each section 396.3cm long (13′)

2 Untitled Maquettes

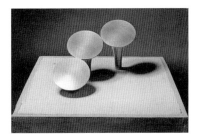

Untitled Maquette

1 9 6 9

Gazebo Maquette

GAZEBO 1969 (Edition of 5)
H 244cm x W 305cm (8′ x 10′)

Enclave Maquette

ENCLAVE 1969
3 units each constructed of 6 sections 366cm long (12′)
Overall L 1677cm (55′)

GAZEBO   **ENCLAVE**

1 9 7 0

ELEVATION 1970
L 183cm x W 183cm x H 24cm (72″ x 72″ x 9½″)

RECOIL 1970
L 210cm x W 22cm x H 27cm (82¾″ x 8¾″ x 10¾″)

INVERSION 1970
274.5cm x 98cm x 91.5cm (108″ x 38½″ x 36″)

Restrain Maquette
24cm x 55cm x 63cm (9½″ x 21¾″ x 24¾″)

RESTRAIN 1970
236cm x 120.5cm x 91.5cm (93″ x 47½″ x 36″)

LIBERATION 1970
L 426.8cm x W 121.9cm x H 213.4cm (14′ x 4′ x 7′)

CORNER PIECE 1970
457.2cm x 457.2cm x 91.5cm (15′ x 15′ x 3′)

FLOOR PIECE 1970
L 510cm x W 230cm x H 10cm (201″ x 91″ x 4″)

The Travellers Maquette

THE TRAVELLERS 1970
H 519cm (17′)

LIBERATION

CORNER PIECE

THE TRAVELLERS

1 9 7 1

Inspan Maquette (Edition of 2)
30.5cm x 74cm x 16.5cm (12″ x 29″ x 6½″)

Square Piece with Rope Maquette
L 52.7cm x W 52.7cm x H 10.2cm (20¾″ x 20¾″ x 4″)

TRIAD 1971

Several Maquettes of Rope Sculptures
Each length approx 366cm (12′)

Untitled Maquette
5 pentagons 22.5cm diameter (8⅞″)

INSPAN 1971
274cm x 20.5cm x 61cm (108″ x 8″ x 24″)

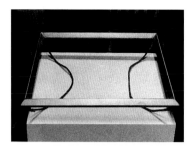

Square Piece with Rope Maquette   **TRIAD**

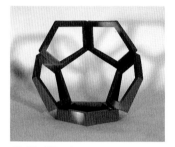

Untitled Maquette

1 9 7 2

Suspension Maquette
35.5cm x 41.3cm x 41.3cm (14″ x 16¼″ x 16¼″)

SUSPENSION 1972
H 157.5cm x W 157.5cm x L 162.6cm (62″ x 62″ x 64″)

Sky Hook Maquette (Edition of 2)
35cm x 31cm x 31cm (13¾″ x 12¼″ x 12¼″)

SKY HOOK 1972
175cm x 183cm x 102cm (69″ x 74″ x 40″)

Series of 22 'Walls' Montages:

1. 6 Steps
2. Hole in the Wall (Edition of 2)
3. Garrison Wall
4. Harbour Wall
5. Barbed Wire (remade 1977)
6. Fern Street
7. School Wall (Graffiti)
8. Torn Wallpaper (remade 1978)
9. Crack
10. Lot 47
11. Brick Walls (remade 1978)
12. Sheep
13. Warehouse
14. Viaduct
15. Rebuilt (remade as Railway Wall)
16. Boundary Wall
17. Earls Court
18. Dockland
19. Railway Wall
20. Turning Point
21. Brick Walls (Scaffolding)
22. Demolition

Each 76.2cm x 57.2cm (30″ x 22½″)

Sail Maquette (Edition of 2 or 3)
H 40.7cm (16″)

Octo Maquette
H 30.5cm (12″)

Untitled Maquette (Interwoven Circles)

SKY HOOK

'Walls' Montages

1973

Timepiece Maquette (Edition of 12)
32cm x 40.5cm x 40.5cm (12½" x 16" x 16")

TIMEPIECE 1973
366cm diameter (12')

Trail Maquette (Edition of 2)
14.5cm x 73cm x 32cm (5¾" x 28¾" x 12½")

TRAIL 1973
183cm x 35.5cm x 46cm (72" x 14" x 18")

Transom Maquette (Edition of 2)
14cm x 73cm x 32cm (5½" x 28¾" x 12½")

TRANSOM 1973
244cm x 76cm x 51cm (96" x 30" x 20")

VERSUS 1973
L 244cm x W 121.9cm x H 76.2cm (96" x 48" x 30")

SLING 1973
250cm x 56cm x 20cm (98.4" x 22" x 7.8")

Contravene Maquette (Edition of 2)
34cm x 48cm x 37cm (13¼" x 19" x 14½")

Retention Maquette (Edition of 2)
73cm x 30.5cm x 13.4cm (28¾" x 12" x 5¼")

Square Piece Maquette (Edition of 2)
31.8cm x 41.3cm x 41.3cm (12½" x 16¼" x 16¼")

Impetus Maquette (Edition of 2)
68.6cm x 41.3cm x 41.3cm (27" x 16¼" x 16¼")

Balloons Maquette
34cm x 15cm x 15cm (13½" x 6" x 6")

Octo Working Model
Full-size

Havering Unit Maquette

HAVERING UNIT 1973-7

TRAIL

SLING

TRANSOM

VERSUS

Contravene Maquette

1974

OVERHANG 1974
107cm x 244cm x 28cm (42" x 96" x 11")

RETENTION 1974
52cm x 320cm x 102cm (20½" x 126" x 40")

VECTOR 1974
107cm x 274cm x 16.5cm (42" x 108" x 6½")

TORSO 1974 Stone Carving
27cm x 16cm x 18cm (10½" x 6¼" x 7")

MYTHICAL BEAST 1974 Stone Carving

OVERHANG

RETENTION

VECTOR

1975

Contravene II Maquette (Edition of 4)
53cm x 52.5cm x 46cm (21" x 20¾" x 18")

Poise Maquette
49cm x 33cm x H 86.4cm (19¼" x 13" x 34")

POISE 1975
320cm x 183cm x 122cm (126" x 72" x 48")

DOCKSIDE 1975
237.5cm x 146cm x 30.5cm (93½" x 57½" x 12")

Pillar Dial Maquette (One Time, One Place)

DOCKSIDE

1 9 7 6

CURVED PIECE 1976-9 (Edition of 5)
L 84cm x W 17cm x H 42cm (33″ x 6¾″ x 16½″)

Book Spine Maquette (Edition of 5)
L 47cm x W 55cm x H 17.5cm (18½″ x 21¾″ x 7″)

Crossbow Maquette (Edition of 5)
L 46cm x W 46cm x H 14cm (18″ x 18″ x 5½″)

Acclivous Maquette (Edition of 3)
68.5cm x 21.5cm x 24cm (27″ x 8½″ x 9½″)

Dockside Maquette (Edition of 3)
49.5cm x 31cm x 31cm (19½″ x 12¼″ x 12¼″)

Oblique Maquette (Edition of 4)
37cm x 37.5cm x 32cm (14½″ x 14¾″ x 12½″)

Flight Maquette

Brick Knot Maquette
H 9cm x W 30.5cm x L 30.5cm (3½″ x 12″ x 12″)

Aluminium Column Maquette

Aluminium Tall Loop Maquette
H 74cm x 10cm x 10cm (29″ x 4″ x 4″)

SAND CASTLE

BRICK LOAD

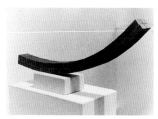
CURVED PIECE

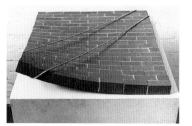
Book Spine Maquette

Crossbow Maquette

Acclivous Maquette

Dockside Maquette

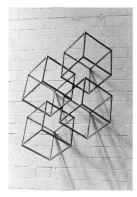
Brick Knot Maquette

BRICK LOAD

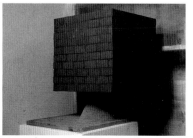
SAND CASTLE

---

1 9 7 7

Equatorial Sundial Maquette
30.5cm diameter (12″, scale 1″:1′)

Veer Maquette (Edition of 6)
42cm x 30.5cm x H 21.6cm (16½″ x 12″ x 8½″)

Oblique 2 Maquette (2 made)
37cm x 37.5cm x 32cm (14½″ x 14¾″ x 12½″)

Box Kites Maquette
H 85.3cm x W 62.6cm x L 45.4cm (33⅝″ x 24½″ x 17⅞″)

Brick Knot Maquette (Edition of 3)
L 55cm x W 50cm x H 42cm (21¾″ x 19¾″ x 16½″)

BRICK KNOT 1977-8
H 213cm x L 358cm x W 231cm (84″ x 141″ x 93″)

Knot Maquette
Scale 1:20

Brick Maze Maquette
Scale 1:20
Maquettes for brick installations at Annely Juda
Gallery, one-man Show (1978-9)

Link Maquette
Scale 1:20

BRICK KNOT

Brick Knot Maquette

Box Kites Maquette

1 9 7 8

BRICK ARCH 1978
H 256.5cm x L 183cm x W 71cm (101″ x 72″ x 28″)

CROSSBOW 1978
304.8cm x 304.8cm x 76.2cm (120″ x 120″ x 30″)

UNTITLED (ROOF SECTION) 1978
256.5cm x 183cm x 71cm (101″ x 72″ x 28″)

UNTITLED (BRIDGE SECTION) 1978
H 42cm x 53cm x 11cm (16″ x 21″ x 4½″)

Balance I Maquette

Series of Slate and Aluminium Maquettes

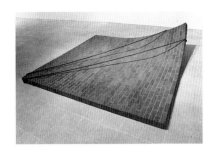

CROSSBOW

Balance I Maquette

1 9 7 9

Brick Aeroplane Maquette
Unfinished. L 48cm x W 43cm x D 8cm (19″ x 17″ x 3¼″)

STILL LIFE 1979 (Edition)
(Bottle and apple)
26.5cm x 25.5cm x 26.5cm (10½″ x 10″ x 10½″)

FRUIT STAND 1979 (Edition)
26cm x 21.5cm x 18.5cm (10¼″ x 8½″ x 7¼″)

EGGS 1979 (Edition)
32cm x 11cm x 18.5cm (12½″ x 4¼″ x 7¼″)

Brick Circles Maquette
Unfinished

Counterpoise Maquette
W 38cm x H 34cm x D 33cm (15″ x 13½″ x 13″)

COUNTERPOISE 1979-80
H 213.5cm x L 152.5cm x W 244cm (7′ x 5′ x 8′)

OCTO 1979-80
H 296.5cm (13′)

Gemini Maquette
W 14cm x L 11cm x H 7.6cm (5½″ x 4¼″ x 3″)
9cm (3½″) diameter discs

Versus Maquette (Edition of 6)
41cm x 41cm x 21cm (16″ x 16″ x 8¼″)

Counterpoise Maquette

COUNTERPOISE

Versus Maquette

OCTO

1 9 8 0

Sentinel Maquette
Original version (with legs together).
H 36cm x W 22cm x D 13cm (14″ x 8½″ x 5″)

Sentinel Maquette
Final version. 36cm x 22cm x 13cm (14″ x 8½″ x 5″)

SENTINEL 1980-1
H 610cm x W 396.5cm x L 235cm (240″ x 156″ x 92½″)

Brick Column Maquette
Unfinished

Compass Bowl Maquette
Scale 1:100

COMPASS BOWL 1980
Installation. Diameter 20.12m (66′), H 3.66m (12′).
Area of wall 216.56 sq.m. (2331 sq.ft.).
Area of base 317.31 sq.m. (3416 sq.ft.) (exclusive of subways)

Sentinel Maquette

COMPASS BOWL

1 9 8 1

EQUATORIAL SUNDIAL 1981-2
Diameter 366cm (12′)

CANTERBURY RELIEF 1981
235cm x 213cm x 15.2cm (92½″ x 84″ x 6″).
Approx weight 800 lbs.
Horizontal scale 1:10,000 (approx 6″ to 1 mile).
Vertical scale exaggerated by factor of 8

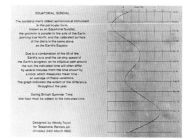

1 9 8 2

Opus Maquette
Original working maquette.
L 42cm x H 29.2cm x W 23.5cm (16½″ x 11½″ x 9¼″)

Opus Maquette
Including model of building. Scale 1:20

Opus Maquette
L 42cm x H 29.2cm x W 23.5cm (16½″ x 11½″ x 9¼″)

ESSENCE 1982
H 213.5cm x L 152.5cm x W 244cm (7′ x 5′ x 8′)

Shell Form Maquette (for marble)
W 43cm x H 26.5cm x D 32cm (17″ x 10½″ x 12½″)

Untitled Maquette (Hourglass/Loop)
H 43cm x 29cm x 29cm (17″ x 11½″ x 11½″)

Untitled Maquette (Entwining Columns for Marble)
H 93cm x W 40cm x D 32cm (36½″ x 15¾″ x 12½″)

Opus Maquette

ESSENCE

Untitled Maquette

1 9 8 3

Untitled Maquette (Silver Circles)
H 28cm (11″)

Network Maquette
25.4cm diameter sphere (10″)

GAZEBO 1983
H 244cm x W 305cm (8′ x 10′)

BRONZE MEDAL
For E.S.A.B.

OPUS 1982-3
L 229cm x W 129.5cm x H 157.5cm (90″ x 51″ x 62″)

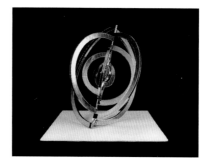

Untitled Maquette

GAZEBO

1 9 8 4

NETWORK 1984-5
305cm (10′) diameter sphere containing an interconnecting
network of aluminium tubes culminating in 720 holograms

Spirit of Enterprise Maquette
H 34cm x 14cm x 14cm (13½″ x 5½″ x 5½″)

Geo I and Geo II Maquette
Scale 1:10

Spirit of Enterprise

GEO I

120

1 9 8 5

GEO I AND GEO II 1985-6
Two tondos each 244cm (8') in diameter

Balance II Maquette
H 63.5cm x 30cm x 30cm (25″ x 11¾″ x 11¾″)

DOCKLANDS BUSINESS ENTERPRISE AWARD 1985

Models for Basildon Underpasses Phase I 1985-8
Various scales plus full-size templates

Models for Basildon Roundacre Scheme Phase I 1985-8
Scale 1:100

EQUATORIAL SUNDIAL 1985
61cm diameter x W 52.7cm x H 55.2cm (24″ x 20¾″ x 21¾″)

Roundacre Scheme

Models for Basildon Underpasses

1 9 8 6

Globe Sundial Maquette
Original maquette with arm.
20.3cm diameter x H 12.1cm (8″ x 4¾″)

Pharos Maquette
Scale 1:12

PHAROS 1986
H 762.5cm x W 410cm (300″ x 165″). Weight 3.346 tons

Nexus Maquette
47cm x 35cm x 33cm (18½″ x 13¾″ x 13″)

NEXUS 1986
L 198cm x W 178cm x H 178cm (90″ x 70″ x 70″)

Landscape Maquette
Scale 1:15

LANDSCAPE 1986
L 1006.5cm (33')

Tree of the Wood Maquette
Scale 1:12

TREE OF THE WOOD 1986
H 289.5cm (114″)

GEMINI 1986
L 29.2cm x W 21.6cm x H 21cm (11½″ x 8½″ x 8¼″)
with 17.8cm discs (7″)

Globe Sundial Maquette

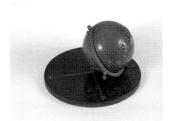

PHAROS

NEXUS

GEMINI

1 9 8 7

Globe Sundial Model
101.5cm diameter sphere (40″) with 213.5cm diameter base (7')

GLOBE SUNDIAL 1987
101.5cm diameter sphere (40″) with 213.5cm diameter base (7')

Armillary Sundial Maquette
30.5cm diameter (12″). Scale 1:12.

The Whirlies Maquette
Scale approx 1:50

Pilot Kites Maquette
Scale 1:20

Pilot Kites
Complete model including buildings. Scale 1:100

GLOBE SUNDIAL

**Armillary
Sundial Maquette**

Pilot Kites

Untitled Maquette (Silver Cubes)
H 34.3cm x W 20.3cm x L 8.3cm (13½" x 8" x 3¼")

Ceres Maquette
Scale 1:12

CERES 1986-7
H 381cm (150")

Spirit of Enterprise Maquette
56cm x 26cm x 26cm (22" x 10¼" x 10¼")

SPIRIT OF ENTERPRISE (DOCKLANDS ENTERPRISE) 1987
H 793cm (26')

Silver Fountain Maquette
H 27cm x 14cm diameter (10½" x 3½")

Stained Glass Window Maquette
With part building. Scale 1:20

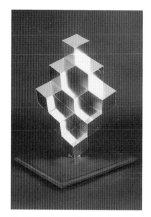

Untitled Maquette

SPIRIT OF ENTERPRISE

1 9 8 8

The Whirlies Maquette
38.1cm diameter (15")

The Whirlies Model
Complete roundabout.
Scale 1:100. 80cm x 62.5cm (31½" x 24½")

THE WHIRLIES 1988
5 spheres each 244cm in diameter (8')
Overall size of roundabout 80m x 62.5m (262½' x 205')

PILOT KITES 1988
2 kites each 300cm x 259cm x H 701.5cm (118" x 102" x 276")

Jester Maquette (Edition of 6)
H 53.3cm x W 34.3cm (21" x 13½") Scale 1:8

ROUNDACRE IMPROVEMENT SCHEME Phase I 1985-8
Environmental Design for Basildon, Essex,
including underpasses (shape, tiling design, etc),
paving, layout, landscaping

SILVER FOUNTAIN 1988
H 228.6cm (90"). Base diameter 137cm (54")

Fireflow Maquette
Including model of building. Scale 1:20

FIREFLOW 1988
H 223.5cm (88")

The Whirlies Model

Jester Maquette

SILVER FOUNTAIN

ROUNDACRE

1 9 8 9

ARMILLARY SUNDIAL 1988-9
3.66m diameter (12'). H 4.27m (14')

Sheffield Sundial Maquette
H 22.3cm x W 24.2cm x L 22.9cm (8¾" x 9½" x 9")

PHAROS II 1989
H 762.5cm x W 410cm (300" x 165")

Phoenix Maquette
27cm x 17cm x 17cm (10½" x 6¾" x 6¾")

Full-size templates for Animal Fresco, Basildon

Continuum Maquette
Scale 2:3

CONTINUUM 1989-90
H 106.6cm x W 121.9cm x L 109cm (42" x 48" x 43")

President Moi Monument Model
Design of building

ARMILLARY SUNDIAL

Animal Fresco

BARKING NORTHERN RELIEF ROAD
Environmental design

BUILDING OF THE YEAR AWARD 1989
Design of Award

Oxide Maquette
280cm x 280cm x 215cm (11″ x 11″ x 8½″)

OXIDE 1989-90
42cm x 42cm x 32.2cm (16½″ x 16½″ x 12¾″)
Bayer 'Colour in Architecture' Award

CONTINUUM

President Moi Monument

BUILDING OF THE YEAR AWARD

1 9 9 0

GLOBE SUNDIAL II 1990
101.6cm (40″) diameter sphere on 205.7cm (81″) diameter base,
10cm (4″) deep

Square Piece Maquette
Working maquette for Plano. Scale 1:12

PHOENIX 1989-90
H 708.6cm (279″)

Rope Circle Maquette
Scale 1:12. 20.3cm in diameter (8″)

ROPE CIRCLE 1990-
284.4cm diameter (112″). Work in progress

ROUNDACRE IMPROVEMENT SCHEME Phase II 1989-90
Environmental Design for Basildon, Essex, including underpass,
paving layout, landscaping and precast animal fresco
incorporating 19 life-size animals cast in concrete covering
7924cm (260′), weighing approx 140 tons

CARDIFF BAY 1990
Environmental Design for Cardiff Bay Public Realm Study Team

BUTTERFLY MOSAIC 1990
L 883.9cm x H 152.4cm (29′ x 5′)

A13 Trunk Road 1990-
Goresbrook Scheme, Barking. Proposal for environmental
design of subways at Renwick and Gale Street including
pedestrian route for Goresbrook Sports Centre, Barking.
4 basic models and 1 full model. Scale 1:100

BUILDING OF THE YEAR AWARD 1990
Design of Award

A13 Trunk Road Models

GLOBE SUNDIAL II

1 9 9 1

SHEFFIELD SUNDIAL 1991
400cm diameter (13′)

SQUARE PIECE 1990-1
45.7cm (18″) diameter tubes forming a 365cm (12′) square
H 457cm. Weight approx 4½ tons

Anchorage Maquette
85cm x 35.5cm x 33cm (33½″ x 14″ x 13″)

ANCHORAGE 1991
H approx 900cm (30′)

BUILDING OF THE YEAR AWARD 1991
Design of Award

Balance Maquette (Edition of 2) (reversed)
H 46cm including base (18″)

1 9 9 2

JESTER 1991- (unfinished)
H 426.8cm x W 274.4cm (168″ x 108″)

SHEFFIELD SUNDIAL

SQUARE PIECE

DRAWINGS, PRINTS, ETCHINGS, PAINTINGS

1964 - 5

Drawings
Numerous drawings and paintings on canvas
Mostly relating to sculptures

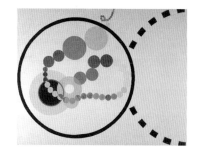

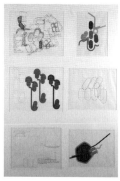
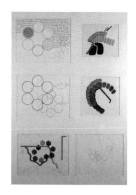

1966

Drawings
Window mounts
Prepared for Sainsbury Award
each 56cm x 81cm (22″ x 32″)

Drawings
Two untitled sketchbook mounted drawings
each 44cm x 55cm (17¼″ x 21½″)

Etchings
Several early etchings including:
Morning 29cm x 12cm (11½″ x 4¾″)
Leo 23cm x 19cm (9″ x 7½″)
Milkweed
Regents Park Zoo
Autumn Leaves

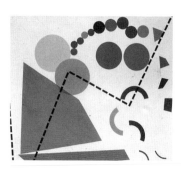

Window mounts

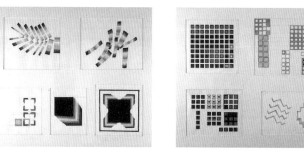

Two untitled sketchbook mounted drawings

1 9 6 7

Prints
Complementary to the **Series** sculptures:
Spring I (Edition of 8)
Summer (Edition of 8)
May (Edition of 8)
September (Edition of 8)
Spring II (Edition of 12)
all approx 62cm x 40cm (24½″ x 15¾″)

Print
Untitled
(Blue, Black and Cerise Squares) (Edition of 6)
58cm x 58cm (23″ x 23″)

Print
Untitled
(Pink, Stone Squares)
60cm x 58cm (23½″ x 22¾″)

Print
Shreds (Edition of 6)
65cm x 51cm (25½″ x 20″)

Paintings
Numerous untitled paintings
Mainly based on **Series** sculptures
152.5cm x 152.5cm (5′ x 5′)

May

September

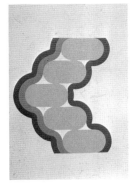

Spring

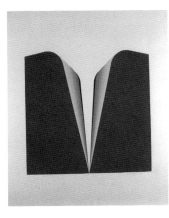
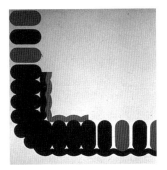
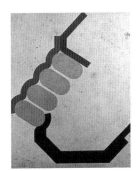
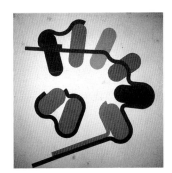

Numerous untitled paintings

---

1 9 6 8

Print
Overland (Edition of 12)
56cm x 58cm (22″ x 22¾″)

Print
Verge (Edition of 15)
52cm x 47cm (20½″ x 18½″)

Print
Calendula (Artist's proofs)
68cm x 54cm (26¾″ x 21¼″)

Print
Square Projection I (Artist's proofs)
68cm x 68cm (26¾″ x 26¾″)

Print
Square Projection II (Artist's proofs)
68cm x 68cm (26¾″ x 26¾″)

Print
Square Projection III (Artist's proofs)
68cm x 68cm (26¾″ x 26¾″)

Print
Square Projection IV (Artist's proofs)
68cm x 68cm (26¾″ x 26¾″)

Print
Square Projection V (Artist's proofs)
68cm x 68cm (26¾″ x 26¾″)

Print
As I Walk through the Trees (Edition of 12)
52cm x 63cm (20½″ x 24¾″)

Print
Remembrance (Artist's proofs)
68cm x 68cm (26¾″ x 26¾″)

Perspex Print
Elipses (Edition of 4)
47cm x 47cm (18½″ x 18½″)

Elipses

Verge

125

1 9 6 9

Drawings
Series of Gazebo Drawings
each 51cm x 61cm (20″ x 24″)

Print
Square Projection ¼ (Artist's proofs)
68cm x 68cm (26¾″ x 26¾″)

Perspex Print
Square Formation (Edition of 2)
51.5cm x 51.5cm (20¼″ x 20¼″)

Perspex Print
'2' (Edition of 1)
51.5cm x 51.5cm (20¼″ x 20¼″)

Perspex Print
Square Projection (Edition of 1)
51.5cm x 51.5cm (20¼″ x 20¼″)

Perspex Print
Elliptic (Edition of 2)
61cm x 51.5cm (24″ x 20¼″)

Perspex Print
Column (Edition of 4)
51.5cm x 51.5cm (20¼″ x 20¼″)

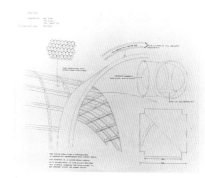

Gazebo

---

1 9 7 0

Perspex Print
Chain (Edition of 1)
51.5cm x 51.5cm (20¼″ x 20¼″)

Perspex Print
Chain II (Edition of 2)
51.5cm x 51.5cm (20¼″ x 20¼″)

Drawing
Untitled Rope Drawing
72.5cm x 55cm (28½″ x 21½″)

Perspex Print
Elevation (Edition of 2)
51.5cm x 51.5cm (20¼″ x 20¼″)

Perspex Print
Triambic (Edition of 1)
51.5cm x 51.5cm (20¼″ x 20¼″)

Perspex Print
Tier (Edition of 2)
51.5cm x 51.5cm (20¼″ x 20¼″)

Perspex Print
Schema (Edition of 1)
51.5cm x 51.5cm (20¼″ x 20¼″)

Perspex Print
Inverse (Edition of 2)
51.5cm x 51.5cm (20¼″ x 20¼″)

Perspex Print
Polytope (Edition of 1)
51.5cm x 51.5cm (20¼″ x 20¼″)

Drawings
Four untitled Drawings
of **Sphere** sculpture
each 72cm x 54.5cm (28½″ x 21½″)

Drawing
Enclave
76cm x 56cm (30″ x 22″)

Lithograph
Print of Sculpture Drawings
used for Axiom Gallery Poster

Drawings
Series of Drawings
related to **Chain** pieces and **Recoil**, etc.
each 76cm x 56cm (30″ x 22″)

Drawing
Ferdie Cat Drawing
30.5cm x 20.5cm (12″ x 8″)

Untitled Rope Drawing

Tier

Schema

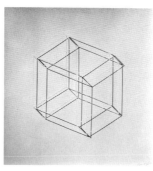

Polytope

Four untitled Drawings

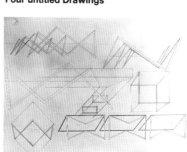

Enclave

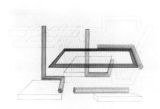

Series of Drawings

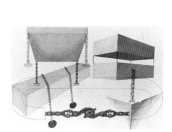

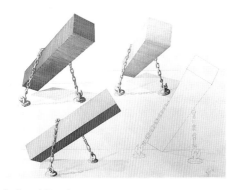

Ferdie Cat Drawing

Series of Drawings

---

1 9 7 1

Drawing
Anchor and Pipes
72cm x 51cm (28½" x 20")

Drawing
Square Piece with Rope
75cm x 56cm (29½" x 22")

Drawings
Series of drawings of Dock Machinery
76cm x 56cm (30" x 22")

Drawing
Triad I
76cm x 56cm (30" x 22")

Drawing
Triad II
76cm x 56cm (30" x 22")

Print
Allotments (Artist's proofs)
76cm x 56cm (30" x 22")

Perspex Print
Allotments (Edition of 1)
76cm x 56cm (30" x 22")

Dock Machinery

Square Piece with Rope

---

1 9 7 2

Drawing
Bollards
76cm x 56cm (30" x 22")

Drawing
Untitled (Gasworks)
76cm x 56cm (30" x 22")

Drawing/Collage
Series of untitled drawings/collages
each 76cm x 56cm (30" x 22")

Series of untitled drawings/collages

Untitled

Bollards

1 9 7 3

Print
Flute (Artist's proofs)
52cm x 47cm (20½" x 18½")

Drawing
Timepiece Shackle Detail
76cm x 56cm (30" x 22")

Drawing
Timepiece Mounting Detail
76cm x 56cm (30" x 22")

Drawing
Timepiece Markings Detail
76cm x 56cm (30" x 22")

Lithograph
King Henry's Yard, E.1 (Edition of 33)
76cm x 56cm (30" x 22")

Drawing
Sheffield Drawing
76cm x 56cm (30" x 22")

Drawings
Havering Unit Drawings
(Measurement drawing + Series)

Timepiece

King Henry's Yard

Sheffield Drawing

1 9 7 4

Drawing
The Drill
74.5cm x 56cm (29¼" x 22")

Print
Tesselation (Artist's proofs)

Print
Mosaic (Artist's proofs)

Print
Cross-stitch (Artist's proofs)

Drawings
Flight
Copper Drawings
55cm x 74cm (21½" x 29")

Lithograph
'Watched'
King Henry's Yard, E.1 (Artist's proofs)
Mounted 53.5cm x 41cm (21" x 16")

Drawing
The Nestlers
Design for children's park furniture

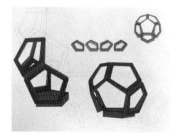

Flight

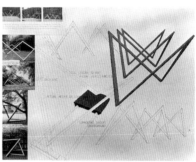

The Drill

1 9 7 5

Drawing
Beyond Square Piece
Drawing with silkscreen
76cm x 56cm (30" x 22")

Drawing
Square Piece
76cm x 56cm (30" x 22")

Drawing
Rope
76cm x 56cm (30" x 22")

Square Piece

Beyond Square Piece

Rope

Drawing
Wire Rope
76cm x 56cm (30″ x 22″)

Drawing
Rigging
76cm x 56cm (30″ x 22″)

Drawing
Sky Hook
76cm x 56cm (30″ x 22″)

Drawing
Yard Sling
76cm x 56cm (30″ x 22″)

Drawing
Pulley Block
76cm x 56cm (30″ x 22″)

Perspex Print
Column II (Edition of 10)
51.5cm x 51.5cm (20¼″ x 20¼″)

Perspex Print
Interface (Artist's proof)
51.5cm x 51.5cm (20¼″ x 20¼″)

Wire Rope

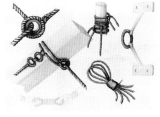

Rigging

Sky Hook

Yard Sling

Pulley Block

1 9 7 6

Drawings
Series of 12 bird drawings:
1. **Emu**
2. **Kestrel**
3. **Tit**
4. **Seagull**
5. **Coot**
6. **Goose**
7. **Ibis**
8. **Owl**
9. **Long-eared Owl**
10. **Jackdaw of Rheims**
11. **Hawk**
12. **Parrot**
each 76cm x 56cm (30″ x 22″)

Etching
13. **Flamingos**

Perspex Print
Ellipse 2 (Edition of 14)
51.5cm x 51.5cm (20¼″ x 20¼″)

Perspex Print
Square Formation 2 (Edition of 4)
51.5cm x 51.5cm (20¼″ x 20¼″)

Perspex Print
Rain (Artist's proof)
46cm x 46cm (18″ x 18″)

Print
Dhow 1 (Edition of 30)
76cm x 56cm (30″ x 22″)

Print
Dhow 2 (Edition of 30)
76cm x 56cm (30″ x 22″)

Kestrel

Tit

Gull

Goose

Long-eared Owl

Jackdaw of Rheims

Hawk

Parrot

Dhow 2

1977

Perspex Print
Polytope II (Edition of 10 – 3 printed)
51.5cm x 51.5cm (20¼″ x 20¼″)

Print
Brick Knot (Edition of 40)
76cm x 58cm (30″ x 22¾″)

Print
Daedalion 1 (Edition of 30)
76cm x 56cm (30″ x 22″)

Print
Daedalion 2 (Edition of 30 – 13 printed)
76cm x 56cm (30″ x 22″)

Print
Daedalion 3 (Edition of 30)
76cm x 56cm (30″ x 22″)

Print
Daedalion 4 (Artist's proof)
76cm x 56cm (30″ x 22″)

Print
Daedalion 5 (3 Artist's proofs)
76cm x 56cm (30″ x 22″)

Print
Daedalion 6 (Edition of 30)
76cm x 56cm (30″ x 22″)

Print
Daedalion 7 (3 Artist's proofs)
76cm x 56cm (30″ x 22″)

Print
Lineate 1 (2 Artist's proofs)
76cm x 56cm (30″ x 22″)

Print
Lineate 2 (5 Artist's proofs)
76cm x 56cm (30″ x 22″)

Print
Lineate 3 (1 Artist's proof)
76cm x 56cm (30″ x 22″)

Print
Lineate 4 (1 Artist's proof)
76cm x 56cm (30″ x 22″)

Print
Lineate 5 (2 Artist's proofs)
76cm x 56cm (30″ x 22″)

Print
Mosque (Edition of 30)
76cm x 56cm (30″ x 22″)

Perspex Print
Cyclone (Edition of 10)
56cm x 56cm (22″ x 22)

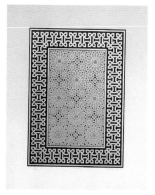

Daedalion 6

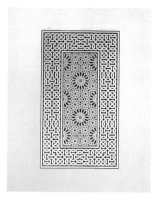

Lineate 1

Mosque

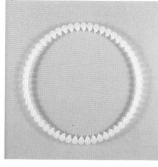

Cyclone

1978

Drawing
Tortoise with Bread
67cm x 46.5cm (26½″ x 18¼″)

Drawing
Tortoise Walking
67cm x 47cm (26½″ x 18½″)

Drawing
Brick Knot
86.5cm x 60cm (34″ x 23½″)

Drawing
Close-up Brick Knot
86.5cm x 60cm (34″ x 23½″)

Drawing
Spine Piece
86.5cm x 60cm (34″ x 23½″)

Drawing
Crossbow
86.5cm x 60cm (34″ x 23½″)

Drawing
Tortoise Walking Away
67cm x 47cm (26½″ x 18½″)

Tortoise with Bread

Tortoise Walking

Brick Knot

Close-up Brick Knot

Spine Piece

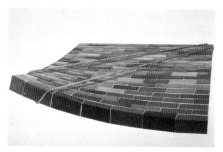

Crossbow

1 9 7 9

Drawing
Fruit Stand
86.5cm x 60cm (34″ x 23½″)

Drawing
Still Life
86.5cm x 60cm (34″ x 23½″)

Fruit Stand

Still Life

1 9 8 0

Drawing
Sentinel
152.5cm x 122cm (60″ x 48″)

1 9 8 1

Drawing
White Rhino Laying Down
67.5cm x 48.5cm (26½″ x 19″)

Drawing
White Rhino Back View
67.5cm x 48.5cm (26½″ x 19″)

Drawing
White Rhino Standing
67.5cm x 48.5cm (26½″ x 19″)

Drawing
White Rhino Captive
67.5cm x 48.5cm (26½″ x 19″)

Drawing
White Rhino Resting
67.5cm x 48.5cm (26½″ x 19″)

Print
White Rhino Laying Down (Edition of 100)
86cm x 61cm (34″ x 24″)

Print
Link (Edition of 36)
57cm x 69cm (22½″ x 31″)

Etching
Tree Walk (Artist's proofs)
30.5cm x 25.5cm (12″ x 10″)

Etching
Seat (Artist's proofs)
30.5cm x 25.5cm (12″ x 10″)

Etching
Little Black Box of Mushrooms
(Edition of 13 boxes, 13 prints in each)
21.5cm x 14.5cm (8½″ x 5¾″)

Etching
Another Mouse (Artist's proofs)
39.5cm x 31cm (15½″ x 12¼″)

White Rhino Back View

White Rhino Standing

White Rhino Captive

White Rhino Resting

Link

Seat

1 9 8 2

Drawing
Drawing for Marble Sculpture
42cm x 58.5cm (16½" x 23")

Drawing
Tortoise Flying Brick Kite
152cm x 122cm (60" x 48")

Drawing
Tortoise with Collapsed Brick Kite
152cm x 122cm (60" x 48")

Drawing
Tortoise with House on Fire
152cm x 122cm (60" x 48")

Etching
Tortoise Flying Brick Kite (Edition of 15)
52cm x 38.5cm (20½" x 15¼")

Etching
Tortoise with Collapsed Brick Kite (Edition of 15)
52cm x 38.5cm (20½" x 15¼")

Etching
Tortoise (Artist's proofs)
29cm x 39cm (11½" x 15½")

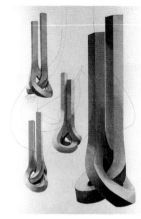

Tortoise

Drawing for Marble Sculpture

1 9 8 3

Drawing
Cayman (Alligator) – London Zoo
152cm x 122cm (60" x 48")

Print
Fruit Stand without Shadow (Edition of 36)
79cm x 58cm (31" x 22¾")

Print
Fruit Stand with Shadow (Edition of 36)
79cm x 58cm (31" x 22¾")

Print
Brick Knot II (Edition of 36)
76cm x 58cm (30" x 22¾")

Print
Egg Box (Edition of 36)
79cm x 58cm (31" x 22¾")

Etching
Culham Bird (Artist's proofs)
28cm x 36cm (11" x 14")

Cayman (Alligator)

1 9 8 4

Perspex Print
Interface (4 Artist's proofs)
52cm x 52cm (20½" x 20½")

1 9 8 5

Drawing
Geese at Bentley
76cm x 57cm (30" x 22½")

Drawings
Spirit of Enterprise
Two original site drawings
each 48.5cm x 54.5cm (19" x 21½")

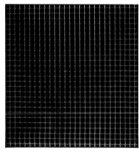

Interface

1 9 8 6

Drawing
Iguana – London Zoo
152.5cm x 122cm (60" x 48")

Drawings
Globe Sundial
Two drawings
each 45cm x 37cm (17¾" x 14½")

Iguana

Globe Sundial

Globe Sundial

132

Drawing
Rope Knots
76cm x 56cm (30″ x 22″)

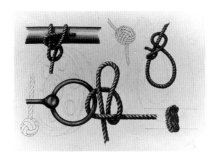

---

1 9 8 8

Drawing
Sheep I
122cm x 84cm (48″ x 33″)

Drawing
Sheep II (back view)
122cm x 84cm (48″ x 33″)

Drawing
Goats
122cm x 84cm (48″ x 33″)

Drawing
Elephant (unfinished)
122cm x 87cm (48″ x 34¼″)

Drawing
Elephant (back view) (unfinished)
122cm x 87cm (48″ x 34¼″)

Print
Sheep I (Edition of 100)
100cm x 75cm (39½″ x 29½″)

Print
Sheep II (back view) (Edition of 100)
100cm x 75cm (39½″ x 29½″)

Print
Goats (Edition of 100)
100cm x 75cm (39½″ x 29½″)

Print
Iguana (Edition of 100)
104cm x 80cm (41″ x 31½″)

Elephant   **Elephant**

---

1 9 8 9

Drawing
Pelicans
101cm x 96.5cm (39¾″ x 38″)

Print
Silk Scarf 'For Rosie' (Limited Edition of 100)
74cm x 75cm (29″ x 29½″)

1 9 9 0

Drawing
Rope Circle on Original Site
63.5cm x 51cm (25″ x 20″)

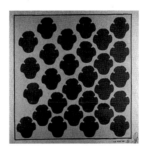

Pelicans   **Silk Scarf 'For Rosie'**

---

1 9 9 1

Print
Owl (Edition of 35)
78cm x 56cm (30¾″ x 22″)

Drawing
Small Owl
70cm x 51cm (27½″ x 20″)

Drawing
Drawing for Gyroscope Sculpture

Drawing
Pygmy Hamsters (Hampstead Ladies)

Drawing
Pygmy Hamster (back view)

Small Owl   **Gyroscope**   **Pygmy Hamster**

---

1 9 9 2

Tapestry
Sheep Tapestry
Dyed wool drawn through canvas
117cm x 167.5cm (46″ x 66″)

Sheep Tapestry

BIOGRAPHY:

1945	Born Stamford, Lincolnshire
1961-67	St Martin's School of Art, London
1980-85	Member of CNAA Fine Art Board
1981-	Member of Royal Fine Art Commission
1982-84	External Assessor London University
1982-	Member of Court of the Royal College
1984-88	Member of Morley College Council
1985-88	Design Consultant Basildon Development Corporation
1985-	Specialist Advisor CNAA
1987-91	Committee for Art & Design CNAA
1988-	Design Consultant Commission for the New Towns
1989-	Design Consultant London Borough of Barking & Dagenham
1989-90	Member of Project Team for Cardiff Bay Public Realm Study
1989-	London Docklands Design Advisory Board
1989-90	Member of Advisory Group of the Polytechnics & Colleges Funding Council

AWARDS:

1964	Walter Neurath Award
1965	Pratt Award
1966	Sainsbury Award
1977	'Duias na Riochta' (Kingdom Prize)
	Gold Medal at the Listowel Graphics Exhibition, County Kerry, Eire
	Arts Council Award
1978	First Prize Silk Screen, Barcham Green Print Competition
1984	Sculpture Competition – Commission, Swansea Maritime Quarter
1988	Sculpture Competition – Norwich Airport
1988	Ordinary Commander of the British Empire
1989	Fellow of the Zoological Society

ONE-MAN EXHIBITIONS:

1970	Axiom Gallery, London
1972	Angela Flowers Gallery, London
1974	24th King's Lynn Festival, Norfolk
	World Trade Centre, London
1975	Annely Juda Fine Art, London
1976	Oxford Gallery, Oxford
	Oliver Dowling Gallery, Dublin
1979	Oliver Dowling Gallery, Dublin
1986	'Building Art – The Process', The Building Centre Gallery, London

GROUP EXHIBITIONS:

1964	Colour Print Gallery, London
	Young Contemporaries, FBA Gallery, London
1965	Sculpture Exhibition, AIA Gallery, London
	Young Contemporaries, FBA Gallery, London
1966	3 New Sculptors, Kasmin Gallery, London
	Sculpture Exhibition, AIA Gallery, London

Experiment in Form, Grosvenor Gallery, London

Upper Gallery, Whitechapel Art Gallery, London

1967 Arlington 2-5, Arlington, Gloucestershire

1968 AIA Prints, AIA Gallery, London

Brighton Festival Sculpture Exhibition, Brighton Pavilion

City of London Festival Sculpture Exhibition, St Paul's Gardens, London

First Burleighfield House Sculpture Exhibition, Buckinghamshire

Artists for Czechoslovakia

First International Print Biennale, Bradford

1968-69 Art for Export, Camden Arts Centre, London

1969 Sculptors at Work, Camden Arts Centre, London

Second Burleighfield House Sculpture Exhibition, Buckinghamshire

Young Printmakers, Museum of Modern Art, Oxford

Sculpture in Transit, Essex and Norwich Universities

1970 Dibujos y Provectos de 16 Escultores Britanicos, Bonino Gallery, Buenos Aires

Graphics 70, AIA Gallery, London

Printmakers Council Travelling Exhibition

Open Sculpture Exhibition, Mid-Pennine Group

Ten Sculptors, Two Cathedrals, Winchester and Salisbury

Walls and Floors, Camden Arts Centre, London

1971 London Now, Messehallen Galerie, Messedamm, Berlin

SPACE, Geffrye Museum, London

Marble Hill Exhibition, Marble Hill House, Twickenham

Serpentine Gallery, London

Art Spectrum, Alexandra Palace, London

1972 A Concept in Multiples, Bluecoat Gallery, Oxford

Print Exhibition, Oxford Gallery, Oxford

Open Field Southern Arts Association, Travelling Exhibition

Art in Steel, Brettenham House, London

1973 Sculpture Drawings, Angela Flowers Gallery, London

Basler Kunstmesse, Basel

Sculpture Exhibition, Globe Theatre, London

Sculpture at South Hill Park, Bracknell

City of London Polytechnic, London

1974 Royal College of Art Galleries, London

Critic's Choice, Arthur Tooth and Sons, London

British Sculptors' Attitudes to Drawing, Sunderland Art Centre, Sunderland

3D Prints Extraordinary, Printmakers Council Exhibition, New Lane Gallery, Bradford

Sculpture in the Open Air, St Matthew's Gardens, London

Drawing Conclusions, Oxford Gallery, Oxford

1975 Sculpture in a Landscape, Marble Hill, Twickenham

1976 Gallery Choice, Scottish Arts Council Gallery, Edinburgh

Sculpture at Worksop, Worksop Priory, Nottingham

Third Eye Centre, Glasgow

Opening Group Exhibition, Oliver Dowling Gallery, Dublin

1977 Listowel Graphics Exhibition, County Kerry, Eire

77th Exhibition of Visual Art, Limerick, Eire

Loyse Oppenheim Gallery, Nyon, Switzerland

The Language of Drawing, Winchester and the Concourse Gallery, Polytechnic of Central London

1978 Hayward Annual, Hayward Gallery, London

Several Travelling Shows in Ireland

1979	Graves Art Gallery, Sheffield
	Edna Reed Gallery, Milton Keynes
	Listowel Graphics Prizewinners, Eire
	Sculptors' Drawings, Minories, Colchester
1980	Leicestershire Collection, Whitechapel Art Gallery, London
1980-81	Leicestershire Collection Travelling Exhibition
1981	British Week, Saarbrücken, Germany
	Second Biennale of European Graphical Art, Baden-Baden, Germany

Work has continued to be exhibited since 1981, however I have chosen to concentrate on working in the field of commissioned sculptures.

FILMS:

1970	Wendy Taylor – Sculpture – Southern Region Television
1988	Half-hour Documentary – South Bank Show – London Weekend Television

PUBLIC COLLECTIONS:

Victoria and Albert Museum, London
Arts Council of Great Britain
British Council International Travelling Collection
Leicestershire Educational Authority Collection for Schools and Colleges
Greater London Council, Golder's Hill Park
Borough of Camden, London
Southern Arts Association
P & O Shipping Lines
City of Christchurch Art Gallery, New Zealand
Guildhall of St George, King's Lynn, Norfolk
Ulster Museum, Ulster
Royal Palace, Qatar
World Trade Centre, London
Gordon Lampart Collection, Eire
Leicester Museum, Leicester
Dudley Museum, Dudley
Lunds Museum, Göteborg, Sweden
Geffrye Museum, London
Ipswich Museum, Ipswich

DESIGN OF AWARDS:

1983	Bronze Medal Arc Art E.S.A.B.
1985	Docklands Business Enterprise Award
1986	"Art and Work Award" for corporate art collection,
	won by B.O.C., organised by Art for Offices
1989	Royal Fine Art Commission Sunday Times "Building of the Year Award"
	Silk Scarf "For Rosie" limited edition for the
	Zoological Society of London
1990	Bayer Award for "Colour in Architecture"

COMMISSIONS:

1969-70	**The Travellers** Lord and Lady Beaumont of Whitley, Hampstead, London
1970-71	**Gazebo** Sir Peter Hall, Wallingford
	William Servaes, Aldburgh, Suffolk
1971	**Triad** Somerville College, Oxford
1971-72	Governor Nelson A. Rockefeller, Tarry Town, New York
1972-73	**Timepiece** The Tower Hotel, St Katharine Docks, London
1977-78	**Calthae** Earl Shilton Community Centre, Leicestershire
1979-80	**Octo** Milton Keynes Development Corporation, City Centre, Buckinghamshire
	Counterpoise Gibbons Dudley, Birmingham
1980	**Compass Bowl** Basildon Development Corporation, Essex
1980-81	**Sentinel** Redland House, Reigate, Surrey
1981	**Canterbury Relief** Wiltshiers Limited for Canterbury, Kent
1981-82	**Equatorial Sundial** Telephone Rentals Limited, Bletchley
1982	**Essence** Milton Keynes Development Corporation, City Centre, Buckinghamshire
1982-83	**Opus** Morley College, London
1983	**Gazebo** Golder's Hill Park, Greater London Council
1984-85	**Network** STC plc, London
1985-86	**Geo I** and **Geo II** NFU Mutual and Avon Insurance Group, Stratford-upon-Avon
1985-88	**Roundacre Improvement Scheme**, Basildon, Essex. Phase I
	to include underpasses (shape, tiling design, etc.),
	paving, layout and landscaping
1986	**Nexus** Curver Consumer Products Limited, Corby, Northamptonshire
	Landscape and **Tree of the Wood** ICI Plant Protection Division, Fernhurst, Surrey
	Pharos East Kilbride Development Corporation, Scotland
1986-87	**Ceres** ICI Plant Protection Division, Fernhurst, Surrey
1987	**Spirit of Enterprise** London Docklands Development Corporation, Isle of Dogs
	Globe Sundial Swansea Maritime Quarter, South Wales
1988	**The Whirlies** East Kilbride Development Corporation, Scotland
	Pilot Kites Norwich Airport
	Silver Fountain BOC Cryoplant Division, Guildford, Surrey
	Fire Flow Strathclyde Fire Brigade Headquarters, Hamilton, Scotland
1988-89	**Armillary Sundial** Basildon, Essex
1989	**Pharos II** East Kilbride, Scotland
1989-90	**Roundacre Improvement Scheme**, Basildon, Essex. Phase II
	to include underpasses, paving layout, landscaping and
	precast animal fresco (250ft total length)
1989-90	**Phoenix** Kelvin Estate, East Kilbride Development Corporation
	Continuum Private Collection, Guildford
1990	**Globe Sundial II** London Zoological Society, Regent's Park, London
1990	**Butterfly Mosaic** Mural, Barking and Dagenham Council
1990-91	**Square Piece** Plano, Illinois
1991	**Sundial** Memorial to Harry Breadley, East End Park, Sheffield
1991	**Anchorage** Salford Quays, Manchester

INDEX OF WORKS

(Illustration references in italics precede page references.)

Artist's Signatures